**Compliments of
Minnesota Children with
Special Health Needs (MCSHN)
1-800-728-5420
Metro Area 623-5150
(Voice or TDD)**

Changed by a Child

Carol and Mark —

Journey with courage,
love, and joy!

Barbara Gill

January, 1998

Changed by a Child

COMPANION NOTES FOR PARENTS
OF A CHILD WITH A DISABILITY

Barbara Gill

Doubleday

New York London Toronto Sydney Auckland

PUBLISHED BY DOUBLEDAY
a division of Bantam Doubleday Dell Publishing Group, Inc.
1540 Broadway, New York, New York 10036

DOUBLEDAY and the portrayal of an anchor with a dolphin are trademarks of
Doubleday, a division of Bantam Doubleday Dell Publishing Group, Inc.

"Crossings" is from *The Book of Medicines* by Linda Hogan, Coffee House
Press, 1993. Used by permission of the publisher. Copyright © 1993
by Linda Hogan.

"Bein' Green" by Joe Raposo, © 1970 by Jonico Music, Inc. All rights
reserved. Used by permission.

Book design by Jennifer Ann Daddio

Library of Congress Cataloging-in-Publication Data
Gill, Barbara, 1946–
Changed by a child : companion notes for parents of a child with a disability /
Barbara Gill. — 1st ed.
p.   cm.
Includes bibliographical references.
1. Parents of handicapped children—Psychology.   2. Parents of handicapped
children—Attitudes.   3. Affirmations.   I. Title.
HQ759.913.G55   1997
649'.15—dc20   96-35826
CIP

ISBN 0-385-48242-6

Printed in the United States of America

September 1997

First Edition

1   3   5   7   9   10   8   6   4   2

for Harjinder, Amar, and Samsher
because we live it together

Contents

Of all the types of success, the most widespread is successful parenthood; the species survives because this is so.

—CLARA CLAIBORNE PARK, *THE SIEGE*

Introduction

I lay looking out the window from my bed in the maternity ward of a Minneapolis hospital on a Monday morning in the last week in March. The sky was leaden and the ground was covered with dirty snow. The dead, gray scene reflected my deep despair. Just the day before I had been told that my new-born son, Amar, my first child, most likely had Down syndrome. On Sunday I had felt numb disbelief. But today I knew that it was true. I see myself, as if in a movie, going home, carrying the baby. I walk up the steps and in through the front door, which closes behind me. And there the film stops, with the picture of a brown house and its blue door. I cannot see what life is like inside the house or what I will do when—if—I come out again. Like a thwarted, hurt child saying, "I won't play" or "I won't eat," I thought, "I'll never practice law again"; "I'll never give another dinner party." I thought, "I don't want to belong to the world of the retarded."

My husband, Harjinder, and I were each thirty-two years old and in excellent health. I had had a normal pregnancy, doing all the right things—good diet, exercise, vitamins, check-ups, rest. No one in our family had ever had a baby with any kind of birth defect. The lecture at childbirth-preparation class about something being wrong with the baby had been for someone else. We were completely devastated by what had happened.

Our lifeline was Amar himself. He was healthy and beautiful, as satisfying to hold as any baby, the sugar sack of weight fitting so naturally in the crook of my arm, the sweet-smelling, fuzzy head, the utter vulnerability of the pulse rising and falling in the fontanel. And of course he was as helpless and demanding as any baby, needing to be fed, bathed, changed, held. Most important, he was ours.

In the first days after learning the news about Amar, Harjinder had been more rageful than I, more insistent that there was a mistake. Our last day in the hospital he asked the pediatrician, one scientist to another, what the odds were that the chromosome tests would confirm that Amar had Down syndrome. Eighty percent, came the answer. After the doctor left, Harjinder sat on the edge of my bed and held my hand. Tears shone in his eyes as he looked into mine and said, "I guess Amar will be our boy forever." I knew then that we were at the same place. Amar was not the baby we had expected, but he was ours. Whatever journey lay before us we would make together.

We brought our baby home and sent out the birth announcements we had already purchased; they read "A star is born!" I remember struggling with whether to say "Amar *has* Down syndrome" or "Amar *is* Down syndrome," a puzzle that seems preposterous to me now. Friends and relatives came to visit, bearing gifts, condolences, comfort, and encouragement. We were enrolled almost immediately in an infant-stimulation program, and in addition to baby care the days were filled with in-take meetings, assessments, therapy sessions, and visits from the public health nurse. The busyness of these early weeks distracted me from my grief, but I was reminded of it every morning when I woke with the familiar heavy feeling in my chest. Somehow I found the time and will to complete the questionnaire from our childbirth-education class. I described our feelings of shock, disbelief, and incredible sorrow, and although I wrote that "Amar's new life deserves celebration," it

2

would be a long, long time before that belief was not shadowed by sadness.

In the fall I returned to my job at the Minnesota Attorney General's office. A few years later we moved to Texas, where our second son, Samsher, was born. I quit work altogether to care for the boys. As the years went by, Amar moved from an infant program to an early childhood program. We returned to Minnesota, where he began public school. Life went on, and it was a normal family life but one always complicated by Amar's disability, with all its consequences and implications, ranging from chronic ear infections to disagreements at school to having a two-year-old who could talk better than his six-year-old brother.

Parents of children with disabilities often compare their experience to riding an emotional roller coaster. It's a good analogy, and as I consider the seventeen years of our life with Amar, I find myself drawn to a related image, that of a spiral. As the years with a child go by, the same intense emotions recur—the sudden, unexpected drops into rage and grief, as well as the upswings into relief, joy, and love. The issues and tasks repeat—we do too much work with too little sleep, struggle to maintain a balanced life, confront a health crisis, or celebrate some small accomplishment. But each time, we do so on a different level. Times change, our child changes as he grows, and our journey changes us, so that how we negotiate the tenth coil is different from how we rounded the second one.

As I have traveled the spiral of our lives I've made gains that have stayed with me. I have learned that our experience is not simply personal, but that social paradigms, politics, and economics shape Amar's life and ours. I am aware that political activism can change those circumstances and I know how to participate in the powerful grassroots movement to secure the civil rights of people with disabilities. I no longer believe, as I once did, that Amar has to be separate because he is different, or that he can live or learn or work only with others like himself, under the guidance of specially trained people. I understand that power is never ceded but must be seized, and that Amar himself has the most potent vision of his future.

On every level I have learned, and learned again, to "go with the flow," to let Amar show me what he needs and what will work. I've learned to appreciate who he is and meet him on his own terms. I've learned to trust my instincts and to be happy with our life as it is. I have learned to let him grow up: Amar is no longer a boy, and his father and I will not be here forever. Every day I feel my love for Amar and his for me. I am proud of the young man he has grown up to be and I take joy in his loyalty, affection, and mischievous wit.

But on every level of the journey I have also had to experience its negative aspects. On each round I wade again through pain and sorrow. I slip into letting Amar's problems—or the world's problems with him—obscure his beauty. I give way to rage, frustration, and self-doubt, turning up the volume on what others are saying and losing the voice of my own heart. At each turn I have fought good fights and picked bad ones, both at home and out in the world. On every level of the spiral I have had to find a new beginning of happiness and acceptance, and to rediscover the need for inner sustenance. Again and again I make my way back to what I somehow knew at the outset, that Amar's life deserves celebration, and back to the larger truth, that each life and all of life must be celebrated.

My greatest challenge arose in the spring of 1987, when, following Amar's disastrous first-grade experience, Harjinder and I determined that he should be in a regular classroom at our neighborhood school. Although our district officials were reluctant, they agreed to the change, and Amar started first grade over again that fall, climbing on the bus with the other kids in our neighborhood. Through this action I was drawn into the inclusion movement, which I hadn't known existed, and there found confirmation and support for many of my own ideas. The people I was meeting—educators, advocates, and other parents—also stretched my thinking as they articulated dreams bolder than those I had dared to have for Amar.

As that first year unfolded it sank in on me that gaining Amar's admission to the classroom was only the first step. There were many problems to be solved along the way. Amar was the first student in our district with Down syndrome—the first student considered mentally retarded—to be fully included. We were the ice-breakers. Many people were being asked to make a big change, and they were uncomfortable with it. There was open opposition and even hostility on the part of some teachers and parents. Amar's teacher was willing and highly experienced, but she had never done anything like this. Just having an aide in her room was new. Even though we had the advice and support of our lawyer, an inclusion consultant, and others, ultimately we were on our own in working with the school and getting along in our community.

Effectively including Amar was neither easy nor quick. In spite of fabulous successes on his part—he learned to read and passed the standardized reading test at the end of first grade—it was tempting for everyone to focus on where he fell short. His speech was hard to understand and his behavior was sometimes over the edge. He painted on other kids' clothes, hid under his desk when frustrated, and did not understand that when the teacher asked, "Would you please read now, Amar?" it was not acceptable to answer, "No." Each succeeding year meant a new teacher, a new team, new issues. We were caught up in a huge personal and institutional change. Many times I questioned whether we had chosen the right course and wondered whether we would have the stamina to follow through on our decision.

Because of my experience with Amar and my activities in the inclusion movement, I began to get invitations to speak to parents and educators. Eventually I left my job as an attorney and worked as a consultant and trainer. Everywhere I went I talked to parents—mostly mothers—who were fighting battles at school. I fell into the trap of thinking that I had to be the "expert," to provide answers as they shared their situations and frustrations. But so often what I could offer seemed to be of no help. Frequently what I said was answered with "Yes, but." When I thought about that "but" from my perspective as a parent, I knew what was on the other side of it: the need for encouragement and for acknowledgment of how complicated, difficult, and lonely the task was. There were no easy answers or quick solutions. There wasn't a right way to do it. No matter what problem each family was trying to solve for their child, they had to decide what they wanted and what they were willing to do to achieve it, and then had to hoe that row each day. People could give us advice, information, and encouragement—and those were all important—but they couldn't do the job for us. The parents I was meeting did not need analysis or argument. They needed what I myself wanted: validation and support.

Continually advocating Amar's inclusion and working in the field threw me back on my personal resources in a way that was new to me. Never before had I been called on to consistently express my beliefs in the face of opposition, and to act on what I believed every day with my own child. I had argued cases to juries, judges, and the state supreme court; how much harder it was to argue my child's case to my neighbor or the school principal! I had accepted Amar as he was, but I found I could not accept society's attitudes toward him. I could not accept—deep down—that I had to fight and convince people of what seemed obvious to me. I was constantly enraged by what I perceived as hostility, stupidity, and institutionalized discrimination, especially in the very organizations mandated to serve his needs. As the years went by the constant struggle depleted me, and by the time Amar was in the fourth grade I had become seriously depressed.

Initially, proper medical care, including medication, brought me out of the depression. Then I saw that I had to deepen my internal reservoirs and develop habits that would continually refill them. I knew I had to find a new response to issues related to disability, to develop emotional perspective. I needed to feel the legitimate anger that moved me to work for change without succumbing to self-destructive rage.

A friend brought me to a twelve-step program. Here I learned what until now I had not effectively gleaned from any therapy, support group, workshop, or book: to let go, to look at my part in relationships, to work on changing what I had the power to change—myself—and to listen, to refrain from judging, to forgive, to attend to my spiritual life. I started to practice yoga and found that its concepts reinforced and provided a physical analog for the twelve steps. Through both, I learned that when I need help I can reach out, but first and last, I have to go in.

I know that other parents of children with disabilities are traveling their own spirals and are regularly knocked off track by many things—a health crisis, a thoughtless comment by a teacher, resistance on the part of a bureaucrat, disapproval from a family member. I've written this book to help people with the "coming back" part of the journey, to offer parents a source of support that does not represent another demand, a place to find reassurance that doesn't expend energy but increases it. I wanted to share what it took me so many circles to learn on my own; to put into words what we experience both in our homes and out in the world; and to set down for easy reference the reminders that help us find and sustain the confidence, strength, and hope to do our job.

The examples and stories in this book are based on real-life situations, although all the names have been changed, and many instances have been fictionalized or blended together. I have attempted to convey experiences of disability from across the spectrum, but I know that I have not begun to represent its many faces. Furthermore, since my own experience is with Down syndrome, children with Down syndrome appear more frequently in the stories than those with other disabilities. Although I believe this book can be useful to anyone who is close to a child with a disability, I have addressed it specifically to parents. Most children with disabilities have their parents as caretakers, and it is the experience I know best.

I have had some struggles with language as I wrote, for the word "disability" covers a range of phenomena that are not only complex, but incredibly diverse and variable, and occur along a continuum. As we know so well, the many labels denoting various disabilities often tell us little to nothing about the unique individuals who bear them. One of John McPhee's geologists, speaking of geologic theories and how they break down under analysis, says, "But when you get down to details you get down to discrepancies." When we talk to each other, parent to parent, we always get down to details. When we use the term cerebral palsy or tuberous sclerosis, we know it is a bare beginning to the real conversation. We talk about whether Tina can read and what kind of wheelchair Nathan uses; we ask whether Chris has a sleeping problem, too; and how do *you* respond to tantrums. We get down to the details and inevitably we get down to the discrepancies, the necessary distinctions between our children, no two of whom are identical.

This book is not intended to be read once, front to back; as the title says, it is meant to be a companion, something to have with you, to read as and when you wish. Accordingly, it is neither necessary nor important to read the entries in any particular sequence. Nevertheless, in an effort to provide some shape to the book, I have grouped the meditations into three categories. Selecting the entries for the first section, "In the Beginning," was easiest, for the crucial issues of the early days and years with a child with a disability are obvious and much the same for everyone. For this section I asked myself what I wanted to say to parents who are just beginning the journey or are still in the early stages.

The second and third sections were more difficult, for the problems, insights, and responses that one has over the years do not occur in a neat progression, but, like our children, follow their own paths and timetables. What is history for one parent whose child is fifteen may be news for another family with a child of the same age. Nevertheless, I have organized the second section as "Rounding the Curves," and included pieces on what parents may experience, and what they may want to think about, once they are over the big hump of acceptance and adjustment and are firmly established in their everyday routines. In the last section, "Transformed," I have grouped pieces that in one way or another look ahead, either to a deeper level of political or spiritual awareness, or to the changes that occur as our child grows. To return to the image I used earlier, the book, like the parents' journey, moves in a spiral. Topics and themes recur, but on different levels and from different perspectives.

Each meditation is headed by a quotation. When the person quoted is disabled or has a relationship to someone who is, I mention that fact. When the quotation is from my interviews or notes, I identify the source and the relative only by first name, each changed to protect people's privacy. When the quotation is from a published work in which the speaker is fully identified, I include the name, and also that of the relative, if the latter is identified in the writing. I have quoted widely from books about disability with the aim of introducing readers to some of the excellent literature that is available. I have also quoted from other sources, ranging from novels to newspaper articles, because I think it helps to remember, or to discover, that our experiences *are* connected to those of other people, and that we can find words and ideas relevant to our lives in many places. All of the published sources of quotations are listed in the Source Notes at the end of the book.

No book about disability can ever match or completely mirror the huge, detailed mosaic of "children with a disability" and their families. I only hope that the examples and stories I have included, and what I have said, touch what is universal in our experience and speak to all of us who, in this particular way, have been changed by a child.

PART ONE

In the Beginning

If you bent or folded rock, the inside of the curve was in a state of compression, the outside of the curve was under great tension, and somewhere in the middle was the surface of no strain.

—JOHN MCPHEE, *BASIN AND RANGE*

No matter how it comes to be that we have a child with a disability, for most of us the beginning is a traumatic and wrenching experience. Our insides are torn by such shock, grief, fear, and sense of loss that it feels like death. Our very identity comes under assault as on every side our assumptions and expectations are turned on their heads. At all the points where we touch the outside world—relating to our family and friends, interacting with medical and social service systems, going out in public—we are stretched and challenged. The whole shape of our selves and our lives is being pulled into a new form.

We don't think we can survive these cataclysmic emotions or take on the tasks now required of us, but we do. We have a child to care for, an activity that absorbs us fully and focuses our attention on life and on going forward. Affirmation, love, and hope trickle through to our shattered soul. Thrown back on our inner resources, we find we do have the strength to meet the demands of each day, and in this way, step by step, we get to the other side of our grief in the only way possible: by going through it.

Always the most tangible and central thing is our child herself. We come to accept her on her terms and open ourselves to whatever discoveries and surprises she may lead us to. We may be startled at the ferociousness of our feelings for her. No matter what ideas we held about disability before she arrived, she has changed them.

Our lives are not destroyed, only bent in a new direction; not over, but dramatically reshaped.

New Baby

Take the baby home. Feed him, love him, care for him.

—PEDIATRICIAN, TELLING A MOTHER
HER NEWBORN HAS DOWN SYNDROME

In the space of a sentence our whole world can turn upside down and inside out. We learn that our baby has a disability, and suddenly we are uncertain about everything we think, feel, and do. This includes our sense of self as well as how to take care of our baby.

We learn that our baby is different and we think we have to treat him differently. Or at best we are confused about when to treat him differently and when to treat him as we would any baby. "He sleeps a lot. Is this due to the disability?" "Should I wake him up to feed him?" "They said to keep her stimulated. Should I do these exercises with her every day?" "I don't know anything about spina bifida. I'd better get to the library right away and read everything I can!"

The task of new babies and new parents is to recover from the excitement and trauma of birth. To eat and sleep. To fall in love with each other. This remains true whether the baby has a disability or not. Our shock and grief and any of the baby's urgent health problems are realities we can't avoid, but they don't change the basic tasks. They make them even more necessary. There will be plenty of time to learn about our child's particular problem, to do the extra and different things this baby needs, to engage in the "business" of parenting a child with a disability. Right now we do what parents do with a new baby: love him, feed him, care for him. Rest.

Accident

I have a six-foot three-year-old.

—PETE, WHOSE SON NICK SUSTAINED A SEVERE HEAD INJURY
IN A SKIING ACCIDENT AT SEVENTEEN

Those of us whose children were born with disabilities had to give up our fantasy of a perfect baby. Those of us whose children become disabled owing to accident, illness, or progressive disease have to give up and grieve for a very real child. The bubbly toddler who now cannot speak. The bright girl who will never go to college. The handsome boy whose face bears a livid scar. The ordinary kid whose chances at a regular life are now compromised.

Everything was fine, great. We could see her growing up into the person she was going to be. We allowed ourselves to dream of her musical career, of his wedding day. We waved goodbye as he headed out the door—on his way to the ski trip, the hiking expedition, the dance. We didn't know we were waving goodbye to life as we knew it, to life as he knew it.

Today I will allow myself to remember and grieve for what was, to feel and know our loss.

Child's Pose

The world is round and the place which may seem like the end may also be only the beginning.

Kneel down with your toes pointing behind you, so that the tops of your feet are on the floor. Place your arms at your sides, with your knuckles just grazing the floor. Then, keeping your buttocks on your heels, bend forward until your forehead touches the floor. Relax your shoulders, allowing your arms to rest on the floor. Exert no energy; sink into the posture.

Now you are in the yoga position known as child's pose. Curled, fetal, it is the position of infancy and suits the infantile feelings of vulnerability and powerlessness. It is a fitting position for the helplessness we are feeling. Child's pose is a position of prostration, and certainly we are on our knees, knocked down by events, prostrate with grief. But child's pose is also the instinctive response to pain: knees to chest, self-protective, the back and outer body curled around to shelter the vulnerable belly and vital organs. There is no action in this pose; it is still, quiet, restful. It is the womb pose, the waiting pose, the dark, floating, ready-to-be-born pose. We begin our life in this position and we return there every time life calls us, as now, to be born anew.

Sorrow

My pain felt like water penetrating into sand, soundless, into the core of my being.

—ANCHEE MIN

When our baby was born we lost something we were already in love with—our idea of what she would be. No baby could ever completely fulfill that idea or be that fantasy, but most babies approach or overlap our dream baby, because our dreams come from what we know, from our idea of the norm. A child with a disability was not in our picture at all, except maybe as an occasional fear. We who have a child with a disability lost not only our fantasy baby, but our reliance on having a "normal" baby.

We feel this kind of loss deep within ourselves. It does heal, but it heals around the edges, leaving an open space in our heart. We grow around the scar and the hole in our heart, and they become part of our architecture, part of who we are. But when the wind blows a certain way, we always hear it and feel it. It makes a sad sound. It makes our heart ache.

Fault

Condemnation heals no one.

—L. TOBIN

Many of us feel guilty and somehow responsible for our child's disability. One of the first things a mother thinks on learning that her newborn has a disability is "Was it something I did?" She begins to review her pregnancy, searching for incidents that might explain what has happened. For many parents, maybe most, it was not something they did or didn't do that determined their child's being disabled.

Others of us are haunted by a mistake or accident we feel we could have prevented. Perhaps a medication we took during pregnancy seriously affected the fetus, or we turned away for a moment and our child was hurt.

All parents make mistakes. Most of the time we escape devastating consequences. This time we didn't. We must forgive ourselves, knowing we coped the best we could at the time and that life will go on. We cannot go back and change the past. Constantly reviewing it, asking what if, and blaming ourselves or another punishes us in a way we do not deserve. It contributes nothing to our well-being today or to the well-being of our child and our family.

Today, I will remember that the most useful thing I can do is to live this day the best I can.

Grief

No one ever told me that grief felt so like fear.

When a grievous event occurs, when something happens that cat-
apults us into grief, it cuts us off suddenly and dramatically from
other people. We have been struck by something unexpected, un-
wanted, undesirable. Most of us experienced the discovery of our
baby's disability as a grievous thing, an event that marked us out
and separated us from the group. To be alone in the sense of not
belonging is terrifying.

Our trauma may make us feel disconnected not only from society, but also from time, from the flow of our life. Our past experience with disabilities may be limited, offering only negative images
about what lies ahead. With no useful history to feed a vision of the
future, we are filled with fear. Questions flood our minds: "How
serious is this disability?" "Will she have friends?" "What will happen to my life?" "What will happen to her?"

It is normal to be afraid and to feel alone. Just for today remember that you are not alone; others have walked the road you are on
now. Even though they don't know you, their love is with you.

Affirmation

I was reading a book about angels when I learned that my nine-year-old had Tourette syndrome. That diagnosis blew me away. I felt that what I needed then was an angel to come down and tell me everything would be all right.

—SHARON, WHOSE SON BRENDAN HAS TOURETTE SYNDROME

For most of us angels come in human form. But sometimes our grief or anxiety or sense of isolation prevents us from hearing the angelic messages. We don't take in that there are people around, saying to us in one way or another that it will be all right. One mother, rereading after many years the cards and letters she had received at her son's birth, discovered that each one said, in its way, "You can do it. It will be all right."

To receive comfort from others we must listen and accept their positive messages. We can seek out those people who affirm us. And we can be our own angels, telling ourselves, "It will be all right. It will be all right."

Fate

Can you accept the idea that some things happen for no reason, that there is randomness in the universe?

—HAROLD S. KUSHNER, WHOSE SON AARON
HAD PROGERIA, "RAPID AGING"

Why me? Why did this happen to us? It is one of the first questions we ask once the enormity of the news about our child sinks in. There might be an explanation—genetic abnormality, a problem during pregnancy—but even behind such a reason lies the same question: why? Often, the question recurs. Someone close to us is expecting a baby and we discover we are anticipating the birth with some fear. We say to ourselves, "I hope everything is all right." When the baby is born and everything is fine, we are relieved and happy. Except that a tiny corner of our minds asks again, "Why me?"

There is no answer to this ultimate question. There *is* randomness in the universe. For those of us with a strong sense of a personal God, acceptance of this can be very difficult. We may feel betrayed, even abandoned by God, or question God's love for us. All of us must struggle in our own way to square what has happened with our idea of God and of the universe. Our challenge is to accept randomness. Why did this happen? Because it did. Why me? Why not? Maybe "why" is not a useful question. Maybe the real question is "What now?"

Rage

The process of grief always includes some qualities of anger.

—ELISABETH KÜBLER-ROSS

But some days, it seems, my rage is all that I have left.

—JOSH GREENFELD, WHOSE SON NOAH
HAS DEVELOPMENTAL DISABILITIES

The discovery that our child has a disability is undoubtedly not our first experience in life with grief and anger, but it may be our first such experience of this magnitude. It is as if our emotions had been a modest lake on which we sailed. Now we're on the ocean. We didn't know we could be tossed on such enormous waves of grief or shaken by such fierce storms of anger. We need a bigger boat.

As terrifying and overwhelming as these emotions can be, we need to know that we are capable of navigating the heavy emotional seas. We need not be drowned by them. By paying attention and learning to experience, understand, and respect our emotions, we can build for ourselves a craft that can sail this ocean and weather these storms. Moving from a small sailboat to an ocean-going vessel is no minor task. We have to remember that it will take time. We should not hesitate to seek any kind of help, professional or otherwise, that will help us accomplish the shift.

Today, if I feel engulfed by grief and rage, I will ride the storm; if my boat cannot handle it, I will call for help.

Survival

People always say to me, "How did you survive it?" But you don't have a choice, because you don't die.

—GALE DESIDERIO, WHOSE SON SAMMY HAS HYDROCEPHALY

You feel as if you are going to die. You may even wish you *could* die. But you don't die. You wake up every morning with a heavy black weight sitting on your chest and you think: When is this not going to be here? Is this ever going to go away? But you do not die, and your child does not die. Then you realize that life is going on and you are going to deal with it. You take it one day at a time. Some days you take it an hour, or even a minute, at a time.

You talk. You think. You get help.

You solve each problem as it comes. You take care of your child. You take care of yourself as best you can. You cry. You laugh. You go back to work. Some days you even forget for a while. The baby smiles. One day you wake up with a light, empty feeling in your chest.

Life creeps back. It's very different from what it used to be and different from what you had expected, but you are living it again. You are a survivor.

What Is Important

Every day is a god, each day is a god, and holiness holds forth in time.

—ANNIE DILLARD

In the wonderful schoolroom scene in E. B. White's *Stuart Little*, Stuart has an opportunity to be a substitute teacher for a day. He quickly decides to dispense with the usual subjects in favor of a discussion about "the Chairman of the World," a position that does not exist but ought to. "The Chairman has to have ability and he must know what's important," Stuart says. "How many of you know what is important?" All hands go up and the children name the important things: "a shaft of sunlight at the end of a dark afternoon," "a note in music," "the way the back of a baby's neck smells," "ice cream with chocolate sauce."

You have a child with a disability. It was a shock and a surprise. Life is different from what you expected or planned, and sometimes quite difficult and painful. But the days continue to carry their richness, and you can still experience the important things. The smell of a baby's neck and ice cream with chocolate sauce are there for you. Nothing can take away shafts of sunlight or a note in music.

Story

All sorrows can be borne if you put them into a story or tell a story about them.

—ISAK DINESEN

You hear the sound of your voice explaining what has happened, describing the events in painstaking chronological detail. The person listening wants you to jump to the end. In his tensed body you can hear the questions: So what happened? What's the point? But you need to lay it all out, to say, *Well, first his blood pressure was high, but the doctor said not to worry. And then we noticed he was sweating a lot and drinking all the time. He seemed to eat constantly, but he was very thin. By now it was September. I made an appointment for a physical and we couldn't get in until October. October 12. I remember because it was Columbus Day. And then . . .*

You need to hear your story out loud so that you can make sense of what has happened and what is going on now. You are like a spider, your words the filaments of sound, lines you are spinning to attach the web of your experience to a corner of the world. In this way you connect the thin gauze of this new, incomprehensible event to the solid wall of what your life has been until now. In this way, telling your story heals you.

Living Now

You don't have to see where you're going, you don't have to see your destination or everything you will pass along the way. You just have to see two or three feet ahead of you.

—ANNE LAMOTT

All parents worry about their children's future and see plenty of examples of what they don't want their kids to become. It's human to hope that our child won't be rude like Uncle Dick, or mean, or lazy, or dishonest. When our child has a disability, the negative possibilities may seem more clearly defined and more certain and, most important, more alien. We may never have had a meaningful personal exchange with an adult with disabilities, so we have no way to imagine such an interaction as something other than distasteful, uncomfortable, or frightening. The parent of a toddler with severe brain damage, seeing an adult who is profoundly retarded, looks at his child and thinks, "Will I still love him tomorrow?"

But our child won't be an adult tomorrow. He is not, suddenly, overnight, going to become the shadow on the wall or the monster in the closet of our imagination. And when he is grown, we will not see him as defective or hopelessly dependent, because he will still be our child, someone we have loved, grown with, and come to know, day by day.

I will live today loving my child as he is right now, and not project fearful possibilities in the future.

Magical Thinking

Granny Tulip was in the breakfast room trying to work out a rather complicated knitting pattern. She had made up her mind that if she worked hard at this problem, Appleby would be home before she had finished. It was pure self-comforting superstition, like not stepping on cracks in the pavement. But it was a way of diverting the mind from an unbearable sorrow.

—SYLVIA WAUGH

A little girl out for breakfast with her family asks for waffles, only to be told that her mother has already ordered pancakes for her. "But I want waffles!" she cries out. "No," says her mother. "I am not changing the order. You will have pancakes." The child's lip trembles, tears well up. She sits in deep thought; then her face brightens and she says, "Sometimes waffles turn into pancakes, don't they?"

A mother and father wait days to discover exactly what is wrong with their newborn, who was whisked from the delivery table to surgery and the neonatal intensive care unit. They realize that they are clinging to every scrap of medical information, constantly talking about the few facts they have, hypothesizing and reassembling them in the absence of any concrete information. "I have an awareness," the mother later writes in her journal, "that the point of this meticulous scavenging exercise is not to produce literal meaning, but instead to help create in us a place where the future, whatever it is, can exist."

If I work hard at this knitting problem, my runaway granddaughter will be home before I finish. Sometimes waffles turn into pancakes. If we can collect and master the medical facts, we will understand what is happening to us.

Magical thinking and self-comforting superstitions serve to carry us through disappointment and intolerable sorrow. They provide a means to fill the void created by waiting and uncertainty. Magical thinking creates hope.

Being

Just to be is enough.

—YOGA INSTRUCTOR

There is only one criterion for inclusion. Breathing, life itself.

—MARSHA FOREST

Today, in our society, many voices ask that the lives of certain people be justified: people who are deemed unable to "contribute" or who are "unproductive"; people who "use resources"; people who do not have a "quality" life.

When Richard hears a talk show or reads an article where such sentiments are expressed, he knows the speaker or writer is talking about someone like his son, Seth, who has been semicomatose for seven of his eight years, since receiving the wrong anesthetic during routine surgery.

For many of us it is impossible to avoid seeing that our child could be viewed as one whose life has no value. We ourselves may be struggling with this attitude toward our child. Even if we do not believe that our child's life needs to be justified, we may lack words to answer persuasive-sounding arguments to the contrary. Without these words we feel helpless, defensive, and frightened.

To be is enough. To breathe is to belong to the human race. Our child exists and is as entitled as the next person to life and liberty. Always remembering that, let us welcome him, accept him, love him.

Difference

*His deafness is neither a talisman nor a curse, but something at once
more prosaic and profound: an aspect of himself.*

—LEAH COHEN, WHOSE PATERNAL GRANDPARENTS ARE DEAF

What's wrong with this picture? Which one is not like the others?
Which one doesn't belong? Picking out what's different is a skill we
begin learning as young children. By the time we are teenagers
we've become expert at finding who and what doesn't fit. It's a
useful skill, enabling us to choose the freshest flowers or avoid the
pothole in the road. But it can get in our way when we think about
people with disabilities, leading us to focus on what's "wrong" and
on how they are different from others, and to believe that disability
means "abnormality" and "deficiency." It may lead us to think our
own children can't belong because they are different.

Our child's disability is a reality, but it is only one part of who
she is; it need not define who she is or who we are.

Equality

Like and equal *are not the same thing at all!*

—MADELEINE L'ENGLE

How we struggle with these ideas of difference and sameness! Our child does have differences. We know that and we need the other people who come into contact with her to know that and appreciate the implications of those differences. At the same time we see all the ways our child is just a child, the same as other kids. And we want others to see that, too. Sometimes we may feel as if we are talking out of both sides of our mouths. What *do* we mean?

What we mean is that human needs are both universal and unique, like fingerprints or snowflakes. All human beings are alike in having needs, but unique in what their precise needs are at any given moment. Everyone requires nourishment, but the food that meets the needs of an infant, an adult woman, and an aging man are quite different. When our child has needs that vary to a marked degree from what is perceived as normal, it is unlikely that solutions tailored to the norm will suffice; treating her "like the other kids" will not meet her unique needs. When we ask that our child be treated the same as other children, what we are really asking is that her needs be given the same weight and value as every other child's needs, not that uniform solutions be applied. Equal treatment does not eliminate distinctions; it takes them into account.

On Her Own Terms

When is my kid's best ever going to be good enough?

—CHARLES, WHOSE DAUGHTER JILL
HAS A SEIZURE DISORDER AND COGNITIVE DELAYS

So often it seems that our child's shortfalls, problems, and incapacities are what others pay attention to, single out, and talk about. Every parent has a drawer full of reports, assessments, and evaluations detailing his child's deficiencies. Every parent has attended meetings that opened with a recitation of his child's deficits, offenses, and failures. Each one of us has seen his child's strengths and gifts overlooked in favor of a discussion of what needs to improve.

There will always be that relative or friend who, no matter how long she knows our child, can't seem to accept her for who and what she is. Our child will regularly encounter people, from a new teacher to the checkout clerk at the grocery store, who will fail to appreciate that the way she is behaving is the best she can do. We cannot control or change the nonacceptance of others, but we can influence it, most powerfully through our own example.

We can make it clear to others that our child is doing her best and we expect them to accept her on her own terms. We can strive always to let our child know that we understand that this is her best and that it is good enough for us.

Today, I will recognize, accept, and celebrate my child's best.

Soul

No child is "perfectly" whole in mind, body, spirit, ability . . . nor can any child meet all of a parent's hopes and expectations. Yet there is a wholeness of each and every child, a wholeness that is unique and brings with it a unique set of possibilities and limitations, a unique set of opportunities for fulfillment.

—FRED ROGERS, *MISTER ROGERS' NEIGHBORHOOD*

In his essay about a young woman he describes as having left-right confusion, poor motor sense, a partial cleft palate, degenerative myopia, and cerebral and mental defects, a woman who appeared to him in a clinical testing situation as "damaged and incorrigible," the neurologist Oliver Sacks goes on to tell how he came to know and understand Rebecca in a different way, a way in which he saw her as "full of promise and potential."

It happened when he came upon her in the clinic gardens, where she sat enjoying the spring day. As he walked up to her, she began to express, in short bursts, almost poetic descriptions of the beauty she was experiencing.

"She had done appallingly in the testing—which, in a sense, was designed, like all neurological and psychological testing, not merely to uncover, to bring out deficits, but to decompose her into functions and deficits. She had come apart, horribly, in formal testing, but now she was mysteriously 'together' and composed," he writes.

As he got to know her, Sacks discovered that at the level of symbol and story, Rebecca did have a composed and coherent view of the world. She could not read or write, but she had a poetic vision of the world and a deep spirituality. She could not unlock a door or tie her own shoes, but she could dance smoothly and rhythmically.

Often what others perceive in us as denial or false hope is really our experience of our child's powers, which are not seen by those who are looking for deficits and think they are the whole story. Living with our children every day, seeing them "conduct themselves naturally in their own spontaneous way," we see how they are people according to the capacities they have. We see their souls.

Let us hold, always, this picture of our child in her completeness, even—especially—in the face of those who see her as decomposed, a collection of deficits.

Potential

Now we come to the power of the Sensitive, the Modest, and the Small—a power that all Piglets have in potential, whether or not they do anything with it.

—BENJAMIN HOFF, THE TE OF PIGLET

It has been called the power of helplessness and it is exemplified by the newborn human infant, who comes into the world naked and utterly unable to do anything for himself. The infant's survival depends on others wrapping him in blankets, feeding him, and holding him; and to secure this nurturance the baby has but one thing—his cry. With a penetrating and unbearable wail, known as the infant distress call, the baby summons the soundest sleeping parent to his side to give him what he needs. Vulnerable, small, and helpless as he is, the baby is powerful enough to bring others to him, and powerful enough to cause all the members of the family to reorganize themselves around his existence.

One can look at children who have many limitations and are unable to do many things, who need extraordinary levels of support, from being fed to being carried, and say that they are the weak, helpless, and powerless. Or one can ask: What power resides in this apparent weakness and helplessness? How does this person influence his world? Is it through a penetrating cry that compels attention? Is it through a simple, unwavering logic that demands that others also see the situation in an uncomplicated way? Or is it through a seemingly total dependence that illuminates how interdependent we all are? What is the potential of this Piglet?

Dreams

That's how we deprive our children, when we take away their dreams. The viciousness of this whole thing is that handicapped children are not allowed to dream. See, they're just as disadvantaged as minority children. You're not allowed to dream big dreams. Just let 'em dream big dreams—that's all the freedom they need.

—RIFT FOURNIER, WHOSE LEGS WERE PARALYZED
BY POLIO WHEN HE WAS SEVENTEEN

As expressions of our wants and deepest desires, dreams shape our picture of the future and fuel our will to live. Nightmares, on the other hand, embody our fears and undercut our hopes. When we follow our nightmares, we limit, even turn away from, our lives. But sometimes our dreams can frighten us more than our nightmares, for when we envision and imagine something more, our choices—and our responsibility for action—expand. As Nelson Mandela said, "Our deepest fear is not that we are inadequate. Our deepest fear is that we are powerful beyond measure."

It is important to acknowledge and name our fears, wily creatures that will go underground and sabotage us if we don't call them out and confront them. But first and last it is vital that we dream, for ourselves, for our family, for our child. We need to dream and teach our child to dream, remembering that to deny dreams is to disable the spirit.

Our power is in our dreams. Let me dream boldly, and let me raise a child who is a bold dreamer.

Identity

I was like everyone else—normal, quarrelsome, gay, full of plans, and all of a sudden something happened! Something happened and I became a stranger. I was a greater stranger to myself than to anyone. Even my dreams did not know me.

—N. LINDUSKA, WHOSE LEGS WERE PARALYZED
BY POLIO WHEN SHE WAS TWENTY-FOUR

A child born with a disability integrates it into her identity as she grows, but we who are parents of such a child have an experience akin to that of people who become disabled later in life. Like them, our sense of who we are has been shattered by the advent of disability and the attendant stigmatization. We too feel that we do not know ourselves. And like a body trying to reject an implanted organ, our psyches will try to throw off this new and alien identity. We may experience keen self-doubt and loss of confidence, yet not even realize that these feelings are related to our having given birth to a child with a disability. It may take years for us to appreciate the impact this trauma has had on our personalities and to understand how it has affected our choices and decisions.

A mother who gave up her career to care for her disabled son eventually came to see that it was not only the very real and extreme family demands that led to her choice, but also her loss of faith in herself. A father became aware that he used his work as an excuse to stay distant from his family because his daughter's disability made him feel like a failure as a parent.

It is imperative that we revise our sense of ourselves and forge a new identity both as an individual and as a parent. How we grow, and whether we grow, will depend on what we choose to do in response to the circumstances of our life. For while it is true that there is no growth or change without pain, it is not necessarily true that all pain leads to growth. For many, it leads to despair.

Given time and the cultivation of circumstances that promote growth, we will find an acceptable new picture of the person we could become; we will find a way to become grounded in a new self. Our dreams will know us again.

Shame

There was no terror at the moment when I knew I had crossed the line into permanent darkness. There was only a sudden feeling of shame.

—VICTOR REISEL, WHO WAS BLINDED IN AN ASSAULT

Disability is a stigmatizing condition, and stigma is accompanied by shame, the feeling that we are "wrong" in our very core. Shame is a normal response to what has happened to us, and is one shared by others in our situation.

I will constantly hold in mind that shame distorts my perception of reality. There is nothing intrinsically wrong with me or with my child. We do not deserve to be cast out. We are here, we're breathing, we belong to the human race, and we have the same basic rights as everyone else.

I will recognize and deal with my shame, because I do not want it to poison my life or the lives of those I love.

Complaining

He was getting a little tired by this time, so that is why he sang a Complaining Song.

—A. A. MILNE

Mark Twain quipped, "Everybody talks about the weather, but nobody does anything about it." A lot of stuff in life is like the weather; there's nothing much you *can* do except talk about it. Sometimes you're too tired or too low or just too overwhelmed by a bad day to do anything. Maybe tomorrow you can do something, but not today. Complaining was invented for times like these.

We're not required to be noble, suffering martyrs. It's OK to vent. Sometimes when talking it out, we start to hear ourselves and get a little insight into the situation. Sometimes we just let off steam and relieve the pressure of our frustration. We may even give our listener a more realistic picture of what our lives are like.

Complaining is just a way of asking for some acknowledgment of our problems and some reassurance. Surely we deserve that much.

Watched Child

But by the time he was two, Paul had become the child of troubled, not proud, parenting: a watched child.

—JANE TAYLOR MCDONNELL, WHOSE SON PAUL IS AUTISTIC

There is a children's story about a girl named Polly Polly Huckabuck, whose father was a night watchman: he watched watches in a watch factory. We, too, are involved in multiple levels of watching. From the moment we become aware of her significant degrees of difference, our child is watched: by us, by teachers, doctors and therapists, relatives and friends, neighbors and baby sitters. And we become "watched parents." We are observing ourselves, and others are scrutinizing us. The entire child-parent experience becomes charged with a supraconsciousness and a self-consciousness that make it almost impossible to act as parents in a centered, spontaneous way. The foundation of comfort, confidence, and common sense that every parent needs has been badly shaken in relation to this child.

It is possible to achieve a new equilibrium as parents of a child with a disability, to find, even to create, a comfort zone. We can stop ourselves from heightened, fearful watching of our child, turn off our awareness that others are watching us, and cultivate a sense of ourselves as competent, proud parents.

Today, I will stop watching watches in the watch factory.

First a Baby

I don't think that I really enjoyed the first year of my baby's life. I was so involved in his care, I just, well . . . I just didn't really get involved in the joy of having him. Of being his mother.

—LINDY SOUZA ALLEN, WHOSE SON SEAN HAS CEREBRAL PALSY

The intensive care needs, the medical crises, the grief, and the constant worry can rob us of the joy of our child's babyhood, of our new motherhood or fatherhood. It is a cruel theft, for more than ever we need to experience the compensating satisfactions and pleasures of parenting to get us through the tough times.

Our child deserves to be a baby, a toddler, a first-grader, a teen-ager, an adult. And we deserve to be the parents of an individual at that stage of development, no matter how altered it may be by the disability. We deserve to have a place in our parenting that is pure, relaxed, and joyous.

Let me remember that first and last we are mother and son, father and daughter, a family. I will not let the cloud of disability block the sun of that truth. Birds sing in this experience too, and my child and I deserve to sing with them.

Expressions of Grief

Her grief was dynamic, even when expressed in anger, and she was always busy, angrily busy, working to ease her grief. His sat in him like a stone.

—LARRY WOIWODE

When a child has a disability, parents grieve, but they grieve differently. Even in this most intimate relationship, marriage, we are often isolated in our grief. What's happening inside us is too terrible to tell, too awful to show. The guilt. The rage. The helplessness. The doubt of self, of God.

We experience grief differently from our partner and act on it differently, and watching the other sometimes feels like facing a stranger. *How can he want sex at a time like this? She's so angry I'm afraid to speak to her. He just sits there! He doesn't even help me bring these groceries in. She thinks this is my fault. What good does all this crying do?* Guilt weighs him down like a stone. Grief drives her like a whirlwind.

I will not expect my partner to rage and howl with me. I will not look for my partner to join me in still sadness. We will accept that we do this differently. It does not mean that one of us doesn't care or cares less. It doesn't mean we don't love each other. It doesn't mean that we won't flow together as water again one day.

Spouse

The reason we managed to stay together through it all seems to be the fact that buried under the stress and agony, behind all the walls we had built between us, we genuinely loved each other. In our case, we were able to build from that base. Now we are back to being a very good team.

—MARY PIELAET, WHOSE SON JON HAS CEREBRAL PALSY

The fact of our child's disability seeps into all aspects of our family life like a hidden leak in the plumbing. We keep finding water dripping from the ceiling, but where is it coming from? We keep experiencing conflict or a sense of distance from our partner, and we can't figure out why. After all, we are used to having a child with a disability, and we feel we have adjusted and are coping well; meanwhile, like water soaking into a sound stud, the disability and its effects are leaving their quiet mark on us and on our marriage. Exhaustion, money worries, guilt, and anger stain and strain the relationship.

Today, I will remember that it is not my spouse, my child, or myself who is the problem. The problem is that responding to our child's disability makes an extraordinary demand on our relationship.

I will begin, today, to think of concrete, positive things I can do to offset this demand and the toll it takes on our marriage. Maybe I'll call a marriage counselor. Maybe I'll invite my partner to go out to dinner. Maybe I'll be sure to put my arms around him and say, "I love you." Maybe I will honestly tell her how I feel.

Whatever it is, I will begin. Today.

Grandparents

Grandparents have as hard a time accepting a disability as parents do. In some ways, their job is even harder because they feel double grief. They grieve over the grandchild's handicap, but they grieve even more at their own child's pain. Ironically, this second-level grief often leaves them unable to offer the support that their son or daughter needs so much.

—ROBIN SIMONS

Just when we need them the most, many of our parents let us down. If only we could let our parents know that we need whatever support they can give us, however they can give it . . . We already feel incredibly isolated and cut off from people, and we need to be reassured that this child will not separate us from our own parents. Their grief for our pain is useless if it prevents them from being there for us. We need them to subordinate their sorrow to ours and to the needs of our baby and family. We need them to help us be strong, and we are more likely to be strong and to manage what we have to manage if we have their support. Their assisting us does not mean we are going to fall apart and leave it all to them.

But their love and help can make all the difference in how successfully we adapt to our new life. Perhaps they are in a position to provide some of the concrete things we need: child care, a financial contribution, an extra pair of hands in the house, someone along on the doctors' visits. Surely those things would be appreciated, but our parents' presence, their touch, their words of love are even more vital. We need them to be there.

Today, I will let my mother and dad know how much I need them.

Family Expectations

When I told my mother about Trent she said, "Things like this don't happen in our family."

—SONJA, WHOSE SON TRENT HAS MUSCULAR DYSTROPHY

A group of women participating in a parent-training program sat down to dinner at one of the weekend sessions. They were already eating when Margaret joined them, looking flustered. "Margaret, what's wrong?" someone asked. But when Margaret opened her mouth to answer, the tears began to flow. Her sitter had canceled at the last moment, and her father had grudgingly agreed to take care of her son. Pressed by his reluctance, Margaret had spent most of the earlier hours at the training session making calls to find another sitter. "My dad just won't take care of Josh. He'll take the other kids, but he won't even try with Josh. And really it's not that hard!"

The conversation moved around the table as, one by one, each mother told a similar story. "My parents are very generous with the grandchildren. They each get fifty dollars at Christmas and on their birthdays, but Melissa gets some cheap, childish toy. A stuffed animal or something. And she's nine now!"

"Bob's mother stays with his sister's kids for a week every winter when Sue and Terry go on vacation, but I can't even ask her to stay overnight with Derek. She goes completely helpless whenever she's around him."

"For months after Steven was born my dad told everyone back in Michigan that he was all right."

"Whenever we're at my sister-in-law's house, all I hear is 'No,

45

Jessica. Stop, Jessica,' and someone telling me what Jessica is doing that's wrong. I hate it."

The women ate in silence after the last mother had spoken, but over dessert one of them said, "You know, I've been very angry at my family for not helping me more with Brian, and I thought they were an exception. I believed that other people's families were giving them lots of support. Listening to everyone tonight, I see that disappointments with family members seem to go with the territory when you have a kid with a disability."

Our families don't always meet our expectations. In responding to our child they too struggle with denial, anger, fear, sorrow, and confusion. In our family, as everywhere else, disability sometimes brings out the best and sometimes the worst in people.

Fathers

Owen, four at the time, was unmanageable. I was working on some overdue paperwork, and he was getting more and more under my skin. Finally, completely exasperated, I snapped at Mary, "Will you get that impossible kid out of here?" She responded instantaneously and in kind, "That impossible kid is your kid too."

—CHARLES R. CALLANAN, WHOSE SON OWEN
HAS DEVELOPMENTAL DISABILITIES

The world over, with rare exception, mothers are the primary caregivers for children, and that includes children with disabilities. This imbalance in the time each parent spends with the child and in the nurturing activities each performs can lead to other imbalances. The mother becomes more skilled at caring for the child and in attending to related matters. Because she does it better, she becomes the primary candidate to do whatever needs to be done, from cleaning the tracheotomy tube, to administering discipline, to attending the school meetings. As the parent who spends the most time with the child, and the one who talks to doctors and teachers, the mother may be quicker to absorb the reality of the disability and its implications for the child and the family. She also has more opportunity, as well as the cultural approval, to experience and express her emotions.

Without realizing it, mothers can crowd fathers out. While harboring resentment because their partners are not helping them, they are in fact not making space for their participation. "He doesn't do it as well" becomes a reason for Dad not to do it at all. Many fathers accept this minimal involvement, taking advantage of an opportunity to avoid difficult, boring tasks and painful emotions.

Fathers need to assert themselves and insist on being involved. Mothers should invite fathers in and let them learn at their own pace to care for the child in their own way. Our children need both of us.

Compromise

How much to compromise is a question on which there is no such thing as advice or consolation.

—ALDO LEOPOLD

Compromise greases the wheels of family life. Not only is it impossible for everyone to have his own way all the time; it is also unlikely that the resources of any family, financial or otherwise, will always be sufficient to the needs of all the members. In families where one member has extraordinary needs, this disparity between needs and resources becomes more extreme. If we are going to add a thirty-minute physical therapy routine plus an extra hour of homework every day for our child with a disability, the time has to come from somewhere. If money must go for expensive special equipment, it may not be there for piano lessons or a family vacation. Trade-offs have to be made. Often, legitimate and quite important needs will be neglected because we cannot do it all.

Two things tempt us as parents to put the needs of the child with the disability ahead of our own or those of other family members. One is the anxiety and guilt that push us to do everything possible for this kid. The other is that the things we do for our child are prescribed and are often monitored by professionals. Each time the physical therapist comes, she asks whether we've been doing the range of motion exercises, but no one comes by to check whether Mom and Dad have been out to dinner lately, or whether our three-year-old is getting her bedtime story every night.

Our homes are not laboratories, hospitals, or schools. Our participation is crucial for the success of the therapies and services our child does receive, but it must be consistent with family life, and this means that compromises have to be made. Sometimes the exercises have to give way to the bedtime story.

Amplification

The normal frustrations of modern life are here multiplied and amplified . . .

—E. B. WHITE

E. B. White's description of New York, in his classic essay on the city, applies equally well to family life with a child with a disability: the normal tasks and frustrations of parenting are multiplied and amplified. Everything is at higher volume, and there's more of it.

One parent calls this the DIF equation. The actual incidents and events involved in raising a child with a disability are not, taken one by one, so different, or different at all, from the incidents and events that are part of raising any child. The difference is in the Duration, Intensity, and Frequency of these events multiplied by the Number of Exceptional Issues.

Other kids break an arm or have a serious illness; our daughter has had at least one surgery every year of her life. Other kids sass back or say no sometimes; every time we tell our son to do something, we risk a serious tantrum. All kids like structure and routine; our daughter gets obsessed with her schedule and has to be persuaded and coaxed to make an exception. Other first-graders have a teacher; ours has two teachers, a case manager, two paraprofessionals, a speech therapist, and an adaptive phys ed teacher. Other kids have one area of exceptional need; our kid has five.

We don't live in the City of Parenting; we live in New York.

Fatigue

Sleep is a major problem again. Noah continues to murder sleep. Up at five, jumping and whining and yelping, impossible to quiet. I go around in a stupor all day.

—JOSH GREENFELD, WHOSE SON NOAH
HAS DEVELOPMENTAL DISABILITIES

Many of us suffer from chronic sleep-deprivation. Our child has to be checked and repositioned throughout the night. Or she only sleeps a few hours a night. Or she rocks or bangs her head as she sleeps. The disability has put an end to sleep as we knew it.

Somehow, we get used to it. And sometimes we get so used to it that we forget what a full night's sleep really is. Then something changes and we do sleep through the night. We can't believe what a difference it makes! We discover that when we are well rested, we are not so anxious, decisions are easier to make, we feel more energetic, happier.

In the soliloquy on sleep in *Macbeth*, Shakespeare uses a string of metaphors that emphasize sleep's restorative power. He calls sleep a bath, a balm, a nourisher; it is the second course in the meal of life, a mender that "knits up the ravel'd sleeve of care." Sometimes we can make changes that enable us to get adequate sleep; sometimes we can't. If we are living sleep-deprived, we must remember that we are living "unraveled." We are missing the bath and balm of sleep. Our daily cares are not being knit up and healed in our unconscious as we sleep; we are not being refreshed and restored to the degree we need to be. We may be trying all kinds of things to help us feel better, and overlooking the obvious—we don't get enough sleep.

Maybe today the best thing I can do for myself and everyone I love is to get some sleep.

Hope

If a patient stops expressing hope, it is usually a sign of imminent death.

—ELISABETH KÜBLER-ROSS

Often others seem to feel a special responsibility to puncture our hopes. They say things like "You know she will never learn to read," or "You need to accept that he doesn't know what is going on around him," or "He's doing well now, but he will reach a plateau."

They would say we are in denial, that our dreams are "false hopes," from which we must be protected. God forbid anyone should go around entertaining false hopes! But, in a certain sense, what other kind of hope is there?

Hope is the thing that is willing to take a chance on the future. And who is audacious enough to say what the future will bring? Hope is the capacity to see something on the horizon that we are willing to move toward. If our hope gets us from today to tomorrow, and in that new day we are ready or able to deal with something we thought we couldn't face, then hope has done its job.

There is a worse thing than false hope. It is no hope.

Self-Esteem

I like you just the way you are.

—FRED ROGERS, MISTER ROGERS' NEIGHBORHOOD

On *Mister Rogers' Neighborhood*, his television show for small children, Mister Rogers always looks out at his audience and says, with great affection and sincerity, "I like you just the way you are." We try to behave and speak to our children in ways that communicate that message. We may make a special effort to convey to our child with a disability that we love her just as she is. What about ourselves? Are we withholding some love from ourselves until we're "better," maybe even perfect?

Go look in the mirror. Give yourself a loving smile. Go ahead and say it: I like you just the way you are.

Self-Assessment

Always taste; never apologize.

—JULIA CHILD

The differences in our family, including our child with a disability, can lead us to feel ashamed or "in the wrong." These feelings are easily aroused when our child and our family are professionally assessed and evaluated, and in any situation where our child's behavior and our parenting are under scrutiny, particularly when whoever is assessing us goes beyond professional bounds or treats us in a way that depersonalizes us.

We can strengthen our sense of self and be less vulnerable to shame if we make a habit of examining our own behavior. Conducting such an inventory can be a scary and difficult process, but those who undertake it discover its power. For if we consistently and conscientiously "taste" our lives by exercising our responsibility to evaluate ourselves, we will be less likely to give up that right to others, and we will be freed of the need to explain or apologize for ourselves. When others do judge us, we are less vulnerable to what they say because we already know the truth about ourselves, and we can recognize when they are trespassing on our responsibility for our own moral integrity.

Today, I will remember that I never need apologize for who I am, who our child is, or who our family is.

Asking for Help

Solving problems normally involves change, and change requires effort. To a truly tired person, most "solutions" look like new problems.

—HELEN FEATHERSTONE, WHOSE SON JODY WAS BORN BLIND, WITH HYDROCEPHALY AND CEREBRAL PALSY

We are exhausted by the needs of our child, yet we are called on to make huge changes and to solve all kinds of problems. This is the Catch-22 we run into when we have a child with a disability. The catch is especially onerous when our child is newborn and during times of crisis. We need so many solutions, but the solutions themselves look like problems, further demands on our scarce energy. There is so much to learn, but we are in a survival mode: getting through the day is a great accomplishment. Those things which are most needed—new learning, creative problem solving, change—are the hardest to come by.

Our first priority must be rest. If we have enough rest, then everything else will follow. To ensure this vital rest, we probably will have to get help—another pair of hands in the house. Contrary to popular belief, help is not a luxury, a self-indulgence, or a sign of weakness. It is a necessity. We deserve to have it. So start with the people most likely to say yes, and ask for the help you need.

Today, I will let go of struggling alone in a net that only tightens as I endeavor to break free of it. I will let go of having to do it all by myself and will ask for help.

Collaboration

Mount Everest is so huge, it takes a whole group to climb it.

—SAM, AGE SEVEN, WHOSE SISTER IS MEDICALLY FRAGILE

Raising a child who needs significant levels of support is an extraordinary task. It may take the family plus a whole group of other people to do it: a school team, a county case management team, a medical team, or a squad of personal care attendants. We may have a child whose needs are so complex and significant that *all* these groups are required. Working with teams of people requires attention, energy, and management skills far beyond the norm. Most of us have added these to our usual parenting tasks without thinking much about them because we had to, and have become so used to the extraordinary job we are doing that we take it for granted.

Today, I will take time out to be conscious that I am climbing Mount Everest. I will remember that I need and deserve nourishment, rest, and periods of relief in order to stay the course. I will also remember that I cannot do the job alone.

B.M.B.D. Disorder

The art of being wise is the art of knowing what to overlook.

Margaret lives on an island off the coast of British Columbia with her daughter Jill, who was born without the parts of her brain that enable speech, sight, and movement. In the early years of Jill's life, Margaret got by with trips to doctors on the mainland and home visits from the early-childhood intervention team. When Jill was five the team recommended that Margaret place her in a residential school on the mainland, where she would have a "full array of services." Margaret refused. Not only did she think her daughter needed to be at home with her family, but she had also become disenchanted with conventional treatments. When she told the team that she was keeping Jill at home and undertaking an unorthodox therapy approach that depended on volunteers, the team psychologist told her that she was being unrealistic and emotional and that she had not accepted the extent of her daughter's disabilities.

Margaret's experience is painfully common. For decades parents have reported that professionals often turn away their requests or object to their goals and choices with clichés and truisms about the parents' attitudes and expectations. A mother laughingly calls it B.M.B.D.—Bad Mom Bad Dad—Disorder.

One man says he thinks of these encounters as portages on a northwoods canoe trip. The discounting remarks are just so many mosquitoes. They are maddening, but there is no point in taking the bites personally or getting angry at them. He needs the energy to haul the canoe and carry the seventy-pound Duluth pack. So he

59

applies an insecticide comprising equal amounts of detachment, focus, and faith in his own experience, ties on his lucky deflector neckerchief, and hits the trail, thinking only of the cool lake at the other end.

I will remember that when I differ from the experts or ask a system to change, I am entering heavy mosquito country. When someone attempts to discount me by denying my experience or by applying stereotypes, I will not give that person the power to stop or divert me, but will consider him just another irritating buzz to be brushed aside.

Received Ideas

There have to be people who are ahead of their time.

—DR. JONAS SALK

Just as the ideas society holds in common about children have changed, so have the communal ideas about children with disabilities. In earlier centuries these children were often smothered at birth or abandoned to die in the elements. Fifty years ago parents were urged to institutionalize their children. Today, parents are encouraged and expected to raise their children at home.

When we became the parents of a child with a disability, we had already formed our own mind-set about disabilities, drawn from beliefs and attitudes of our culture. And as we embarked on the task of raising our child, we continued to get the message, sometimes indirectly and subtly, other times explicitly and directly, of what society thought about disabilities and how we should raise our special needs child. *Aren't they lucky to have so many special programs? If you would discipline him, he wouldn't run away from you. We aren't really equipped to accept a child like this. Dear Ann Landers, My dinner was ruined when I was seated next to a boy in a wheelchair who moaned and drooled.* The ways our family, friends, strangers, professionals, and even other parents respond to our child and our situation, and what they say to us, all carry pieces of this communal idea.

But now we may find we don't always agree. Our experience with our child has affected our thinking and our expectations. We begin to see the gaps between the reality we are living and the received ideas, and to perceive the ways in which the social construct is erroneous or inadequate. When we begin to voice these new and different ideas, we are often met with resistance, even ridicule. It is at such moments that we need to remember that we are swimming against the stream, and that "the way things are" is just the way they are *now*, not the way they always were, nor the way they ought to be or have to be.

Today, let me have the courage of my own convictions and experience. Let me have the strength and persistence to swim against the stream if that is what I need to do.

The Public Family

The Way of Self-Reliance starts with recognizing who we are, what we've got to work with, and what works best for us.

—BENJAMIN HOFF, THE TAO OF POOH

To meet our child's needs we often have to apply to government and other agencies for assistance, which brings us under the scrutiny of those entities. Social workers and program administrators may be visiting our home, compiling information, and observing our child and our family. There will be rules and restrictions governing our qualification for and our use of the funds and services we need, and we will find ourselves changing our lives to meet them. Uncle Sam has joined our family in a way we never expected. Sometimes we feel our house is like a doll house in which one wall is missing and our family and our life are always on view.

Most families do not have this level of involvement with outside agencies and professionals. It is important to remember that it is unusual and that we have the ultimate right and the responsibility to decide what is best for our child and our family. We especially need to cultivate self-reliance in the face of a system that often compels us to choose between privacy and services.

I will carefully decide whether or not to accept intrusions into my private life. Are they necessary to secure the services my child and my family need? I will remember that my partner and I must make the final decisions about how we live. Others may have good ideas, but we have to live our life and we know best what will work and what won't.

Politics

All things change when you get political power. Politics changes lives.
—ED ROBERTS, FOUNDER OF THE CENTERS FOR INDEPENDENT LIVING
AND A LEADER IN THE DISABILITY CIVIL RIGHTS MOVEMENT,
PARALYZED BY POLIO AT FOURTEEN

As parents we are under tremendous pressure to be politically active for disability rights, because we know that political action can change and even save our child's life, now and in the future.

When it comes to politics, it helps to ask what kind of politician I am. Am I a grassroots worker, a rabble-rouser, a diplomat, a legislator? Do I work better outside the system or within it? Am I a leader or a good follower? Maybe I am just a good citizen, one who keeps herself informed, votes, and contributes financially.

It's also important to consider what base we have for political action. One activist says, "To be politically active, you have to have security." It may be the security of a solid marriage and good support systems; it may be financial security; it may be the security of a strong organization committed to the same principles.

Once we assess our base and our personal style, we can decide the best way to undertake the political activity so vital to our child's survival and success.

Other Parents

I felt it shelter to speak to you.

—EMILY DICKINSON

We may count among our dearest friends other parents of children with disabilities. We find comfort and validation with others who share our experiences and outlook. It's a relief not to have to explain ourselves, and to feel confident that our child is accepted. It helps to get tips and advice from someone who has been there before us.

But this isn't always the case. Often, the only thing we have in common with another parent is that each of us has a child with autism or that our kids are both in special education; and that isn't enough to sustain a relationship. We find that similar experiences don't necessarily lead to similar responses: what we think is best for our child may differ radically from what another parent is seeking.

Even when our children have the same disability, the differences between the children may be enormous. When the disabilities are different, we may consider the other family's situation completely alien to ours, or we may find ourselves thinking exactly what we fear parents of "normal" kids think about us: "Thank God I don't have *that* to deal with. How do they do it?"

Instead of being able to support another family, we sometimes find the magnitude of their challenges weighing us down. If they experience pain, frustration, sorrow, rage, it may only serve to aggravate these emotions in us. Then, too, talking to other parents, especially in groups, can feel like being in an echo chamber, each horror story eliciting another one. Sometimes seeing into other families is too much like looking in the mirror.

Let me support and learn from other parents as best I can, without assuming that we will like or even understand each other very well. When friendship and understanding spring up, let me appreciate them for the precious flowers they are.

Forgiveness

*My most painful encounters have been with older parents who placed
their child in an institution. I want to say I understand, but I don't, and
I can't quite get over blaming them on some level.*

—JEAN, WHOSE DAUGHTER BRIANNA HAS EPILEPSY

The writer Chip Brown sought out and visited his sister, whom his
parents had institutionalized when he was quite small and with
whom no one in the family had had any contact for many years.
Writing about his experience, he shared his parents' pained responses to his questions about their decisions. "My father once told
me he wondered if his life would have meant more if he had been
more involved with Chris. If he could have seen her handicap as
love's challenge. He did not. Nor did my mother . . . Having
Chris was a 'terrible mistake,' she said. 'She'll hang over me like a
sword until I die.'"

We have all had times, however brief, when we felt that somehow we had personally failed, or that we were caught in a "terrible
mistake" we wished we could blot out of our lives. We have all had
times when our perception of our child momentarily slipped or
shifted, like a holographic picture, and she appeared to us the way
Chip Brown's sister appeared to her family: "We saw how we were
not like her, not how we were the same. We looked at her with eyes
that seized on her freakishness at the expense of her humanity."

We can understand that times change, and our own attitudes
and responses are not expressions of our virtue or superiority, but
result from a changed social and political climate that provides
more support and choices to families like ours. We can understand

that each day we can bring to "love's challenge" only what we are, and it is not always enough.

Today, I stand at the window and imagine the thousands of parents over time who have faced in some form what I face. I send out my love and acceptance for their decisions, their sorrow, their failings, and their strengths. I forgive myself for judging them. And I ask that they forgive me.

Lighten Up

Humor is a prelude to faith and
Laughter is the beginning of prayer.

—REINHOLD NIEBUHR

Read the comics.
Call someone who always makes you laugh.
Rent a funny movie.
Take a deep breath.
Consider the comic aspects of the situation.
Watch Bill Cosby reruns.
Blow bubbles with the kids.
Do whatever it takes, but LIGHTEN UP!

Practice

Practice makes perfect.

—OLD SAYING

I watch my yoga teacher's demonstration. Then I try to assume the crow pose. First I squat, with my feet flat on the floor. Then I spread my fingers and place my hands flat on the floor, inside my legs, as close in toward my body as I can, pressing the outside of my upper arms against the inside of my calves. I keep my head up and my gaze forward. With a flat back I begin to rise up on my toes and move forward until my feet come off the floor and I am balancing on my hands. I glide forward with intense focus. For seconds my toes are off the floor—one inch? two? Then I slip back. I return to the pose. I try again, and then again.

Every time I practice crow, my arms get stronger, my back releases a little more, my quadriceps stretch, my concentration improves, and I am less likely to hear my mind's voice saying "I can't do this!" Every time I attempt crow with full attention, I understand more about my body and more about this pose, as well as more about my body in this pose. That I may never complete and hold the pose is not a reason to stop doing it. The practice is all that matters. Practice does not make perfect. It makes better. It makes stronger. Every time I practice, I am closer to the crow pose than I was before.

Love

In a selfless act, you are serving a part of who you really are.

—ARNOLD BEISSER, WHO WAS PARALYZED BY POLIO
AT THE AGE OF TWENTY-FIVE

The physical acts we perform for our children easily become tiresome chores. Our son is seven and we still have to dress him; at fourteen we are helping with the shampoo, the bath, putting the special lotion on the very dry skin. He is well beyond age one and we are still feeding him and will be for years to come. Through another infection, another surgery, we are nursing, holding, rocking.

There are days when we think we cannot do another feeding or give one more bath. And then there are those moments when we give ourselves completely in response to our child's need. We turn ourselves over to our child and what we are doing. We know the intimacy of placing food in another person's mouth; of sitting by a child's side in the dark, singing, so that he can sleep. We are not just putting on a shirt; we are consciously touching another person with love. When we surrender ourselves to these acts of physical caring, we experience love; we are healed and made strong. Our tasks are our opportunities.

Optimism

Gardening is an exercise in optimism. Sometimes, it is the triumph of hope over experience.

—MARINA SCHINZ

Seven days after the seeds are planted, green beans begin to sprout; they rise out of the earth with their heads bowed, their delicate green necks pushing up through the rough clods of dirt. Even when the earth is dry and hard, the tiny new plants break through. Our kids can seem like those bean sprouts—vulnerable, fragile, and faced with a task that seems too difficult. They undoubtedly need lots of help, some weeding, some water. But they will grow through the dirt to raise their faces to the sun. They are stronger than they seem.

Courage

"You only blinched inside," said Pooh, "and that's the bravest way for a Very Small Animal not to blinch that there is."

Piglet sighed with happiness, and began to think about himself. He was BRAVE . . .

—A. A. MILNE

When your courage fails, look at your child. Watch how hard he works at his homework. Be aware of the effort it takes him to lift the fork to his mouth. Observe the stoicism with which he endures his chemotherapy. Be conscious of the dignity with which he conducts himself in an environment where people are staring at him. Study what he does to make himself happy.

Not even we, who are so close and care so much, can really know what it takes for our child to accomplish just the basics that every day requires. Our kids define the word *brave*. Watching them, can we be any less?

Patience

Patience! Patience! Patience! I pray so hard for it, and then, somehow, it comes.

—DOROTHY, WHOSE SON SCOTT WAS DISABLED
BY A STROKE AT THE AGE OF TWO

Dear God, give me patience.

Hold back my hand from reaching to do something for her before she has a chance to try it herself.

Stop my tongue from interrupting her as she makes her own way through what she has to say.

Release the irritation I feel when I see the food on the floor again.

Calm the anger flooding me because this wheelchair is so damn heavy.

Let me only do my part.

Let me be present for this moment and do what it asks of me.

Nurture

When my granddaughter was born and we learned she would not live a year, my son came home and got his Lionel trains out of the attic. Every few days for the seven months Marci lived he came over to our house and worked on rebuilding that train set.

—ANGELA, WHOSE GRANDDAUGHTER MARCI HAD ANENCEPHALY

Remember the things that comforted you as a child: a familiar song, certain foods, a warm bath, soft flannel, digging in the dirt. One of the pleasures of having children is the opportunity it affords us to return to our childhood awareness of ourselves. We can join our children in listening to Raffi tapes, wrapping up in a blanket for a nap, making tomato soup or tapioca pudding. We make sure these things are part of our children's lives because we know they foster their growth. And when we participate in them we learn that the soothing and comfort they provide can still nurture us. Even when our kids are "too big," we can choose simple, available comforts for ourselves. Especially in times of stress, when we are being asked to grow in ways that tax our capacity for change, we can return to childhood activities and soothe ourselves with a hot bath, heal ourselves by listening to a familiar lullaby.

Understanding Gap

Nondisabled Americans do not understand disabled ones.

—JOSEPH P. SHAPIRO

The understanding gap. You confront it all the time. You're aware of it when someone asks what grade your child is in and you notice her eyes glazing over halfway into your explanation of how special education classes are organized; when someone distances herself from you by saying, "I think you're a saint to do what you do"; when someone discounts your reality by responding to a problem you are having with your child by saying, "But all kids are like that."

So often it seems that people just don't get it. This lack of understanding can be a great source of frustration, pain, and just plain weariness. It's tiring to educate the whole world, and the fact of the matter is that it's impossible. But there are things we can do to ease the stress of living on the other side of the "understanding gap."

We can share our experiences by inviting others into our homes and lives and by honestly telling our story. We can *remember* that people do not understand, even people with good intentions who want to understand. And we can look for what is similar in our experiences and those of another person. There is, for example, a lot of common emotional ground between a man who placed his mother in a nursing home and a man who placed his teenaged son in a group home.

Today, I will seek out and spend time with people who do understand.

Scapegoat

According to psychoanalytical theory, I was responsible for [my child's] handicap. He was a beautiful two-year-old child who didn't speak, showed no traces of emotion in his eyes, appeared to be deaf, and walked on tiptoes. Primary autism was mentioned.

—ANONYMOUS BELGIAN MOTHER, WHOSE SON HAS AUTISM

Historically, women have been blamed for failing to bear a child, for having a girl instead of a boy, and for anything "wrong" with a child. Of course, science has now shown that men as well as women are infertile, that gender is determined by the father's chromosomes, and that autism is a neurological disorder. Nevertheless, the cultural propensity to hold mothers responsible persists, making them the logical targets when blame is assigned.

Generally, when others scapegoat mothers, it is usually to relieve their own feelings of frustration, rage, and helplessness evoked by disability. Yet doing so seriously wrongs women by undermining their sense of confidence and competence as mothers, and contributes nothing to the task at hand, which is caring for and raising the child.

Today, I will accept responsibility for those things I am truly accountable for and refuse to let myself or anyone become a scapegoat.

Tiger Mothers

And so it began—anger, denial, fear, but most of all, fierce love. It has been this fierce, sometimes unreasoning, love that has carried us through the many years since Owen.

—MARY CALLANAN, WHOSE SON OWEN HAS DEVELOPMENTAL DISABILITIES OF UNKNOWN ORIGIN

A reporter interviewing Daphne Gray, whose deaf daughter Heather Whitestone became Miss America 1994, describes her quality of hyperawareness: "A faraway look comes to her eyes when she speaks about what Heather can do, as if she hears something no one else can. As if having a deaf daughter means she hears extra." We mothers know that Daphne Gray *does* "hear extra." As do we. We hear, see, and feel things others don't even notice. Our experience—with its pain, vigilance, and hard work—has heightened our senses when it comes to our child. It is as if we have developed extra nerve endings. We are tiger mothers—ever watchful, ever ready—tireless to protect, provide, defend.

Sometimes we sense that others are wary of us. They feel—and fear—the great power within us, the fire burning in our eyes. We are tuned in to something extra, something they don't hear.

Coming Out

The world is at best ignorant and indifferent, and at worst hostile—we're going anyway.

—CAROLINE, WHOSE DAUGHTER CHELSEA HAS RETT SYNDROME

A lot of what we do relative to our children is motivated by our desire to protect them. The more vulnerable our child is or is perceived to be, the more protective we are likely to be, and usually appropriately so. But often we expend our energy protecting ourselves or the rest of the world.

We have thoughts like: *If I let her wear what she wants, people will think I am a bad mother. His screaming bothers people, so we won't take him there. When she comes along we all have to go slower, and we can't ask others to do that. It's true he can't learn as much as the other kids, so I guess he can't be with them. I won't take him to the mall because it's just too embarrassing to be stared at all the time.*

It is not our job to protect the world from our children. It is our children who are the victims of very bad luck. Other people are not the "victims" of our children, and no matter how hard we work at it we are not going to "fix" this child or make him "normal." It is not unreasonable to ask the world, one small group or one person at a time, to accept him as he is. Neither is it just or moral for society to exclude some of its members because including them takes some work and effort.

One thing is sure. People will never accept our child if we don't ask them to, expect them to, insist they do.

Welcome

You see, lately I've come to understand that although we all begin school as strangers, some children never learn to feel at home, to feel they really belong. They are not made welcome enough.

—VIVIAN GUSSIN PALEY

Our children are among those who are consistently rejected by other children, who are not made welcome enough, who never learn to feel at home at school. Sometimes they don't even get a chance to be with other kids, instead, spending their school careers in special education classes. The effort of educators and therapists always seems to be toward improving them, making up their deficits, making them socially acceptable. We often buy into this idea that if we can just "fix" them enough, they will be likable, they'll become qualified to join the others. But they start from the outside, having to earn their way in.

In time we see that no matter how "good" they get, no matter how much progress they make, how many negative behaviors are extinguished or skills mastered, they will never be good enough. They will never qualify. But the cost of social exclusion is too high. Each and every child needs to be accepted as he is. As Vivian Paley says, "The *group* must change its attitudes and expectations toward those who, for whatever reason, are not yet part of the system."

As a family, and as a society, we must change group attitudes, expectations, and rules. For if any child deserves to belong, then every child deserves to belong.

Medicalese

There was more. Along with his patent ductus arteriosus and his trisomy 21, there was laryngomalacia (floppy larynx), jaundice, polycythemia (an abnormal increase in red blood cells), torticollis, vertebral anomaly, scoliosis, hypotomia (low muscle tone), and (not the least of these) feeding problems. That's a lot of text to wade through to get to your kid.

—MICHAEL BÉRUBÉ, WHOSE SON JAMES HAS DOWN SYNDROME

A 1994 newspaper article on people with Down syndrome repeatedly identified them as "Down syndrome patients." People with Down syndrome and other disabilities often *are* medical patients, especially at the time of diagnosis. On the average they are "patients" more than most people, but they are not *always* patients or *only* patients, any more than is a person with a heart condition or a chronic skin rash. As one father stated, "My son is not his disability."

Not only do most of our children's disabilities include medical issues; the whole realm of disabilities has been "medicalized" in our society. Thus, "disabled" comes to mean the opposite of healthy, and a chromosomal difference like Down syndrome becomes a "disease" or an "infirmity," putting yet another layer of separation between us and our child, between our child and others, between us and other parents. We start to talk about our son or daughter, and within seconds we sound like a medical dictionary. Of course our children have real medical conditions, and we must master the terminology to understand those conditions and to communicate with medical professionals. But we do not have to accept that language completely and unequivocally. We need not let technical language obscure our child's humanness.

Today, I will remember that a disability is a human condition that may have medical aspects.

Labels

Label jars, not people.

—BUTTON SLOGAN

When the case manager introducing the participants at a team meeting for a young woman named Lila gets to Lila's father, he says, "And this is Dad."

A nurse breezes into the examining room where a mother is waiting with her son and asks, "Are we Mom?"

The assessment report comes. It reads: "Subject is a white male, age 17, currently classified as Trainably Mentally Handicapped."

In a university student center we see an office door with the sign DISABLED STUDENT ASSISTANCE.

We overhear a conversation in a restaurant. "He's a spastic," someone is saying.

In the face of the tremendous challenge, threat, and mystery that disability represents, the desire to limit it and control it by labeling is powerful indeed. We daily confront the expression of this desire as we and our child are labeled and categorized. We ourselves may use labels and cling to diagnoses, attracted to the control and certainty they seem to offer.

When we refuse the label and insist on being called by our name, insist on our child being called by her name, we are asserting our personhood and refusing to be reduced by being unnamed.

Deviance

The female is, as it were, an impotent male.

—ARISTOTLE

A first-grader with Down syndrome was working with his dad to correct a worksheet during his first year in a regular classroom. The assignment was to find the synonym for a given word from a list of three other words. They got to the word "different." The choices were "alike," "strange," and "OK." The child had checked "OK." It was marked wrong. The right answer was "strange."

Different gets defined as strange; what is different is identified as deviant. As Carol Gilligan demonstrates in her book *In a Different Voice: Psychological Theory and Women's Development*, early theories of psychological development were put forth by men who unthinkingly took male development as the norm, and thus saw female development where it was different as deviant or inadequate. "Implicitly adopting the male life as the norm, they have tried to fashion women out of a masculine cloth," Gilligan writes. "It all goes back, of course, to Adam and Eve—a story which shows, among other things, that if you make a woman out of a man, you are bound to get into trouble. In the life cycle, as in the Garden of Eden, the woman has been the deviant."

Similarly, the development of children with disabilities has been observed and described in terms of the development of children without disabilities. The children with disabilities are then categorized as departing, or deviating, from the established norm. Because, as Gilligan observes, "it is difficult to say 'different' without saying 'better' or 'worse,' " what deviates quickly becomes "worse"; that is, deviant, strange, wrong, inadequate, in need of correction.

We need to look at who has created the norms. We need to ask whether the problem lies in the definition of the so-called norm, or the very desire to create a norm. Instead of fixing a person, maybe we need to fix the norm or devise a more meaningful one. In our efforts to avoid the label of deviance, we parents are often perceived as denying difference. But we are only struggling to express what that first-grader saw: different is OK.

Missing

*It is easy to slip into a parallel universe. There are so many of them:
worlds of the insane, the criminal, the crippled, the dying, perhaps of the
dead as well. These worlds exist alongside this world and resemble it, but
are not in it.*

—SUSANNA KAYSEN

We need look no farther than our museums, our televisions, our
newspapers, magazines, and movies to understand that people with
disabilities are missing from the picture. The same goes for com-
mercials, comic strips, advertisements, books, catalogs: you rarely if
ever see a child or adult with any disability. If you were an alien
trying to infer the real culture of earth from its representation of
itself, you might never realize that there were millions of people
whose mental or physical functions are different in some significant
way. When these people do appear in the media, they are portrayed
as special, apart, tragic, pitiable, or heroic; that is, as stereotypes.

People whose lives are not touched by disability neither see it
nor are aware of its omission from the representations of the world.
Yet for those of us who are affected, never being in the picture
distorts our perception of ourselves and invites us to believe that we
have no place there. Our sense of self is never quite aligned with
the images of men and women, mothers and fathers, children and
families that are being put forth as the world.

Overcoming our exclusion from the world's picture of itself takes
a double act of imagination: we have to see our invisibility, our
shadowness—see that we are left out, and then we have to imagine
ourselves coming out of the shadows and into the light of our
rightful place.

Questions

Be patient toward all that is unsolved in your heart . . . try to love the questions themselves.

—RAINER MARIA RILKE

What expectations are reasonable?

What should I compromise and how much?

What is the difference between accepting what cannot be changed and settling for less?

How do I use anger to solve problems and not be overwhelmed by that anger?

What is the difference between making useless comparisons with others and seeing things in perspective?

What is the difference between learning from experience and second-guessing myself?

What issues are about me and what issues are about my child?

How do I conduct myself with dignity when I am being wronged?

How do I live today to its fullest?

Failure

In baseball, the very best hitters only get three hits every ten times at bat. And guess who has the all-time strike-out record? Babe Ruth.

—MELBA COLGROVE, HAROLD BLOOMFIELD, AND PETER MCWILLIAMS

We bring the new baby to a family reunion, and our brother won't hold him. We accept the first-ever invitation to a classmate's house for our kindergartner, and she is brought home early because she messed her pants. We enroll our son in a summer school art class, but the teacher says he can't stay in the class after he paints another kid's shirt. We take our daughter, who wears a protective helmet, out to dinner and are seated at a table in the back next to the kitchen. We make special efforts to get our son accepted as a volunteer worker at the local hospital, and after the first day he refuses to go back. It interferes with his TV schedule.

There's a lot of failure to be experienced as we work to find and make places for our children in the everyday world. And it hurts. It's frustrating, maddening, painful. The bad feelings are powerful enough to make us question our belief that our child can attend a certain function or handle a new responsibility, or our expectation that others can accept and accommodate him. These failures are painful enough to make us say: Forget that. No way. Too hard. Hurts too much.

The negative experiences are not definitive. They are not proof that we should not bat. Each one is just a swing and a miss. Even if it's a strike-out, it's not the whole story. It is true that we must experience some successes if we are going to keep on trying things for our children. Sooner or later we have got to get a hit or, yes, we will quit batting. But we might not get one right away. We might not get one for quite a while. We are going to miss. We are going to strike out. We are going to have slumps, but we will never get a hit if we don't get up to bat.

Even in the face of early failure, let me have the faith to keep swinging.

Mistakes

We should be careful to get out of an experience only the wisdom that is in it—and to stop there; lest we be like the cat that sits down on a hot stove-lid. She will never sit down on a hot stove-lid again—and that is well; but also she will never sit down on a cold one any more.

—MARK TWAIN

There are all kinds of mistakes. Big ones. Small ones. Silly ones. The unavoidable. The irreversible. The trivial. The life-altering. The realized-in-hindsight variety and its flip side, the I-saw-it-coming. As parents, we make all kinds of mistakes. But parenting a child with a disability offers even more opportunity for errors than parenting another child. For one thing, we have few if any models. The clues from our cultural context—neighborhood, school, church, the media—often don't apply or don't help. What works with our other children does not succeed with this one. As we make decisions, we are in uncharted territory.

It helps to remember that, for the most part, we have room to make mistakes. Our errors are not going to harm our child permanently unless we persist in them. Even when a mistake does have a serious consequence, the experience has something to teach us. Instead of lingering in regret and self-recrimination, we can pay attention to what that precise lesson is and apply it in the future.

I know I will continue to make mistakes, but from today I will think of them as the whetstone with which I sharpen the cutting edge of my effectiveness.

Crises

You never really know, when a crisis happens, if this will be the one that undoes you, puts you over some undefined edge.

—KATHY SON, WHOSE DAUGHTER LAURA HAS CEREBRAL PALSY AND A
VARIETY OF LEARNING, EMOTIONAL, AND SOCIAL CHALLENGES

In a crisis, adrenaline clarifies our thoughts and floods us with energy. We know what to do and we have the strength to do it; physically, it is a rush, even a high. But repetition dulls this response, and when crises become everyday occurrences there is not enough adrenaline to get us through another race to the hospital in the middle of the night. Family and friends who initially responded to the call of dramatic urgency fall away as the exceptional becomes the commonplace.

Physically and psychically human beings simply cannot sustain living at fever pitch. But our child's medical crises do not pace themselves; the life-and-death events keep coming. As our ability to respond fades, the repeated extreme episodes do not give us jolts of energy; they leave us numb and drained.

One father whose son frequently stopped breathing in the first four years of his life compared the relentless crises to ocean waves. At first, riding the waves, though scary, is exhilarating. But they just keep coming and coming, and you get tired. Eventually the ocean overpowers you: you can no longer ride the waves, you can't stop them from coming, and you can't get out of the water.

Persistent crises put families at risk for illness, addiction, and depression. They create extreme situations that require equally extreme levels of support. No one's interests—not ours, our child's, our family's, or the community's—are served if we drown in the ocean of constant crisis. It is appropriate for us to call for help and worth our effort to secure the support that will let us ride these waves.

Pain

He hadn't known you couldn't enter a child's helplessness with all the skills of adulthood, and make him whole, but had to stand off with the knowledge adulthood brings, helpless, and watch the child suffer and hope that your hopes for him touched another source and returned to him as strength from the Lord.

—LARRY WOIWODE

Dear God,

Give me the strength to be present at my child's pain.

Help me to have faith in his competence.

Help me to be honest with him.

Help me to convey the confidence I have in him.

Spare me the necessity of using force.

Keep me from denying or minimizing what he is experiencing.

Don't let me make my pain more important than his.

Don't let me abandon him in any way because of my own fear and weakness.

Don't let me be overpowered by my frustration and feelings of helplessness.

Remind me that pain is survivable.

Remind me that he knows I would not permit this if it were not necessary.

Help me bear my suffering with strength, dignity, and honesty and so provide an example that will calm and reassure him.

Remind me that my touch, my smell, my presence are all to him.

Help me to stay here beside him.

Amen.

Mortality

Change comes upon us, not slowly, gently evolving, within our control, but suddenly, abruptly, within hours, sometimes moments, the course of our lives so turned around, turned about, inside out—a slick road on the way home from work; in the night, the discovery of a lump.

—FERN KUPFER, WHOSE SON ZACHARIAH WAS DIAGNOSED AT THE
AGE OF THREE WITH A DEGENERATIVE BRAIN DISORDER

The truth is that change occurs both imperceptibly and slowly, as well as suddenly and dramatically. The slow drip of water on stone works a change as real and radical as the lightning bolt that splits and uproots a hundred-year-old oak tree. The long process that compacts our spine and weakens our muscles is as true as the single accident that severs our spinal cord. The slow change occurs through an accrual of moments; the fast, dramatic one can occur in a moment.

Slow, imperceptible change makes it easier for us to maintain the illusion that we are in control of the change or that there is no change, that we are staying the same, that we will live forever, while sudden, traumatic change rips away that illusion in one swift, undeniable stroke. Most of us experience the introduction of disability into our lives as this kind of violent change. We cry out that we are not the same, that we will never be the same again, and mourn the innocent self who lived on the other side of the event.

Our cry for the lost self is a universal cry, the cry of human beings over their mortality, over human life as a process of constant change and loss. For us this loss is writ large, experienced intensely, shoved in our face. Instead of quietly disintegrating over time, the veil of illusion was torn away, and we saw our own mortality. But it is a mistake to think the disability robbed us of our "same" self. Living takes that self regardless. Living changes us, whether subtly, without our notice, or suddenly and harshly; it changes each one of us every day. Our experience is not outside life or different from what happens to others; it is only an intense and rapid experience of the essential human condition.

Placement

Our decision to place her was both right and wrong and demonstrates how perplexing and delicate choices like these are to make and accept.

—DAVID SEERMAN, WHOSE DAUGHTER CASSIE HAS CEREBRAL PALSY
AND PROFOUND DEVELOPMENTAL DELAYS

By the time Kyle was fifteen I couldn't lift him anymore and I was unable to arrange for someone to come into our home to help. I don't think a nursing home is any place for a teenager to live, and I miss my son terribly, but as a single mom I see no other options right now.

I tried to persuade Janet that we should keep Kim at home, but she was adamant, and since she was the one taking care of her, I did not feel I should insist on my way. I have to admit that since Kim has been away Janet is finally coming out of her depression.

When I got divorced in the early seventies the judge made no allowance for Stephanie's disability. I had to go back to teaching to support us, and I had no one to be there when Steph came home from school. It broke my heart when Steph moved to the group home, but I didn't know what else to do.

We managed fine with David until he began to be violent. None of the things we tried in response were working, and after fifteen years we were tired. We prayed and prayed over this decision and we have finally come to terms with it. It has been very hard, but we know it is best for our family.

Russ made it very clear to me: either we placed Mindy or he would leave.

In an era when more and more families are succeeding, with support, in raising and caring for their children at home, the decision to place a child becomes even more painful. Why is it only we who cannot manage? What will others think?

Helen Featherstone notes in *A Difference in the Family* that when she was considering whether to place her son, who was blind and profoundly retarded, in a residential hospital or keep him at home, she felt she was having to choose between appearing to others as a coward or a hero, when in fact she was an ordinary person.

We are all ordinary people, and though many of us are called to make extraordinary decisions, the best response for each of us is the one that our daily life can support, which is something only we can know.

No Strangers

It is because I am one with them that I owe it to them to be alone, and when I am alone they are not "they" but my own self. There are no strangers!

—THOMAS MERTON

It's just you and your child. Until he came into your life, he is what you had always thought of as "other"—strange, different, not you. Now you are alone with him, and he *is* you. He came out of your body. He bears your name. When you gaze into his face, your own eyes stare back at you. Day by day, year by year, he wins you over, brings you around. He changes you. You live intensely with this person who is no longer a stranger to you because he is you and because you know him so well. And, over time, as you go out in the world, you find you are more curious, more tolerant, and less afraid. You see fewer strangers. You come to realize that everyone is different in his individuality and alike in his humanity.

Accommodation

Erosion, giving the land its appearance, is said to be the work of water, ice, and wind; but wind is, almost everywhere, a minimal or negligible factor, with exceptional exceptions like Wyoming.

—JOHN MCPHEE

A relentless southwest wind blows in the Laramie Range of Wyoming. It has blown for eons, scraping the mountains bare of soil, carving out the landscape. It causes trees to grow at an angle and lifts into the air things that ought to stay on the ground. It complicates all manner of human activity. People who live there successfully have reached an accommodation with the wind; some who couldn't, went insane.

Disability is a steady west wind in our lives. It permeates our existence, altering the topography of our days and causing our family and our life to grow at an angle. Without judging the wind as good or bad, we can observe the truth of it, acknowledge the force of it in our lives, and take the measure of our accommodation.

PART TWO

Rounding the Curves

No one, professional or amateur, should underestimate the immense fund of goodness, knowledge, and resourcefulness possessed by ordinary parents.

—CLARA CLAIBORNE PARK, *THE SIEGE*

We make our way through the early stages, the initial drama and shock, and then through the sheer business and busyness of responding to the particular problems our child's disability presents. We emerge from deep grief and think, "There. That's finished." Our family reorganizes itself to accommodate the reality of a child with a disability and we adapt to our new roles, better understanding and adjusting to our altered place in the world. We continue to confront dark sides of this experience and perhaps discover new ones: prejudice, stigma, our own ambivalence toward our child, our anger, our tendency to be overprotective or overcontrolling. We may slip into the role of supermom, noble martyr, or victim. We struggle with self-doubt, and discover that the grief is never completely finished.

But now we may also be able to reflect more on our experience and our responses, and to develop greater awareness and perspective of the meaning of this disability in our lives. We realize that in some ways we are more alone in this than we might have thought, but we also enjoy the other side of that knowledge, which is that we are much more capable than we thought, and that we can and should trust our instincts.

We begin to appreciate the important role our attitude plays. We recognize, consciously or intuitively, that since we must ultimately depend on our own resources, it is vital to keep them replenished. We see that there are gains, but there is no real arrival; that we're part of a process in which there are no ultimate or definitive answers. We shift from asking what is the meaning of life to looking for what in life has meaning, where the happiness lies in every day.

Answers

Ever since we relied on our mothers to make a bruised knee better with a Band-Aid and a kiss, we have held on to the assumption that someone out there, somewhere, can make us better.

—ELLEN J. LANGER

The assumption we formed in childhood—that someone can make us better—carries over to our children and takes on a special sharpness with regard to our "hurt" child, our child with a disability. If we still want someone out there to make *us* better, how much more we want someone to make our child better, or to make our family better. Furthermore, we have a very real need for information about our child and her disability, and for solutions to the myriad problems the disability raises for her and for us. So we are out there, looking, searching, trying to find the answers.

We would do well to examine our search for answers. First of all, what about this idea of "fixing" the disability? If we look at our child as a person with certain characteristics, rather than as sick, diseased, or defective, we are bound to adjust our perception that we need to fix her, that we have to find the right person with the right Band-Aid. We don't need someone to take away the cerebral palsy; we do need help on how to ease the muscle contractures our child experiences. Second, are we assuming that all the answers lie "out there," that other people, very likely "experts," have them?

A lot of answers *are* out there. We learn a great deal by talking with other parents, consulting doctors, and reading books. But we need to find for ourselves the answers no one else can possibly give us; the answers that must be our own to be useful. We can learn a lot of good information about sex from doctors, books, and talking to friends. But can anyone tell us how to make love?

Today, I will have faith in my ability to make my own decisions.

Unhappiness

When you're faced with leukemia everything else is just minor.

—SANDRA BAKUN, WHOSE DAUGHTER JILL HAD CANCER

Having a child with a disability gives us an entirely new scale for measuring what is important. Things that used to worry or make us unhappy now seem insignificant. We find ourselves impatient with the complaints of others, many of which appear minor, even silly.

But unhappiness is a constant in every life. Our golf game got rained out. We tore a fingernail and tomorrow is the big party. The clerk in the store was rude. Our girlfriend didn't call. Things like these really can make people unhappy, as can thousands of other incidents that lie somewhere along a spectrum between the triviality of a torn fingernail and the significance of a disability.

Our child's disability forcefully reminds us of what really matters in life. Yet, by taking away our capacity for mundane worries, it also separates us from the everydayness of life. Ultimately, if our own unhappiness becomes completely tied up with our child's disability, we may feel that we can't be happy as long as our child has a disability, and conversely, believe that if this child is cured, dies, or is gone, all our problems will be solved and life will be good again.

The day we find ourselves unhappy over a torn fingernail or a rained-out golf game is the day we know that we have returned to the ordinary world and our child's disability is taking its place as one part of our life.

Self-Determination

What I think the political correctness debate is really about is the power to be able to define. The definers want the power to name. And the defined are now taking that power away from them.

—TONI MORRISON

People with disabilities and their families understand very keenly what it means to be defined by others. We are defined by being labeled: emotionally disturbed, crippled, deaf-mute. We are also defined by having our experience categorized by others, including those who observe and study us, and the professionals who care for us. These definitions are reinforced by the institutions that provide the services governing our lives. To get what we need, or what our children need, we must "qualify" by meeting the definition.

Part of the outrage we feel at having a child with a disability comes from this experience of being defined by others, or having to submit to, and even cooperate in, having our child so defined. Fortunately, we live in an era when minority groups in America, whether gays and lesbians, people with disabilities, or people of color, are seizing the power to name themselves and define their own experience and lives.

Today, I will remember that I have the right, and my child has the right, to say who and what we are.

Double Standard

In some ways I expect more from Sean than I expect from my other kids.

—TRICIA, WHOSE SON SEAN HAS FRAGILE X SYNDROME

A couple left the team meeting at their son's group home in disgust. The group home manager was concerned about the young man's weight and wanted to change his habit of having two candy bars when he got home from work every day. The team proposed limiting him to one candy bar. His parents were also concerned about their son's weight, but they knew that his candy bars were one of the joys of his life and one of the few things he had a choice about. They couldn't help observing that the group home manager and two other members of the team were also overweight. They felt sure that no one was monitoring what they ate and imposing punishments when they made an unhealthy choice. They were free to be fat.

The parents sighed, thinking how many versions of the candy bar incident they had lived through. When their son was two, the teacher in the early-intervention program said it was time to toilet train him, wrote it as a goal on their son's plan, and taught them behavior-modification techniques. When Tim still had accidents a year later, they felt like failures, until their second, "normal" son was still in his diapers at the age of three and a half. In fourth grade a note had come home from the special education teacher: *Tim is refusing to tie his shoes. When we tie them, he undoes them.* Then, they went to school one day for a meeting and saw that every fourth-grade boy was trailing his laces behind him. Later, in high school, Tim frequently got detention for swearing. Again, typical behavior for adolescent boys.

The rules are often different for kids with disabilities, especially mental disabilities. They are held to ideal standards of behavior and are never allowed to exercise bad judgment. They are not free to be fat or sloppy or rude. As parents, we may buy into applying different standards to our children because we think we are supposed to. We don't have to. We can realize the false logic of a system that says our children's differences are significant enough to justify special schooling and housing and constant supervision, but are not sufficient to merit special allowances and different behavioral standards.

We can apply our common sense and adopt the good habit of thinking about our children in the context of the rest of the human race. What is typical for kids this age? What is tolerated and what freedoms do they have? Are untied shoes in style? Is swearing common in high school? Are half the people in America overweight? If there is a problem here, what part does the disability play and what allowance should be made for that?

As often as not, there is no problem at all, beyond the imposition by adults of unreasonable or unfair standards.

Process

For at bottom, and just in the deepest and most important things, we are unutterably alone.

—RAINER MARIA RILKE

The first thing visitors encountered at an exhibit of artist Jonathan Barofsky's, at the Walker Art Center in Minneapolis, was a painting hung over the doorway to the exhibit. Like a traffic sign in black letters on a yellow background, it said: SLOW DOWN. YOU ARE ALONE. *You have no one to please but yoursel_.* In the painting the word "self" was incomplete; the artist left off the "f."

Barofsky's message may be an injunction to the viewer. Take your time in looking at these pictures. Even if you are in the company of others, you are essentially alone. You can see them only out of your own eyes. It's not a contest. You can—in fact, you must— make your own judgments, which are not subject to anyone else's agreement or approval. You have no one to please but yourself.

The painting may also be a statement of his credo as an artist. Even though we are about to enter a show of his work to look, evaluate, accept or reject, understand or be mystified, praise or condemn, he is telling his viewer that when he made his art he followed his own time table and his own process. In the first and last analysis his judgment is the only judgment. He was alone; there was no one to please but himself.

Finally, it is a simple and profound statement on the existential nature of life. You are essentially alone. Life is in the process, in the living, not in the outcome, and the process of living is the process of making ourselves. Through interaction with our environment, we fashion who we are and who we will be, but we never complete

109

the task; we are in a constant state of becoming. As one woman put it, "When they're about to close the lid on my coffin, then they can stamp FINISHED on my forehead."

Your life is your own work of art. Take your time. You have no one to please but yoursel_.

Attitude

Be not afraid of life. Believe that life is worth living, and your belief will help create the fact.

—WILLIAM JAMES

What our brain says to us matters; it has the power to affect, influence, and even change our attitude and, through that, the outer aspects of our lives. Although our inner attitude cannot change the fact that our child has disability, it can affect the way we perceive and respond to that disability. If our attitude is one of hope and possibility, it will affect our determination to seek out anything that might help our child. Candido Jacuzzi was inspired to invent the whirlpool because he wanted to duplicate at home the hydrotherapy his young son received at the hospital for his rheumatoid arthritis. He didn't cure his son, but he did find a way to provide comfort and relief from pain, and along the way he created something millions have enjoyed.

Most of us won't invent a new therapy, but with an attitude of hope and possibility we will create a better life for our child through such things as a good school, a talking computer, an atmosphere of happiness in our home. We will also create a better life for our family and ourselves, because we have rejected a script that says our lives are now tragic. We have adopted the inner attitude that our lives are OK, sometimes even wonderful. Consequently, the outer aspects of our life, despite hardships and times of difficulty, will be OK. We will have changed the outcome through our attitude.

Awareness

No thoughts, just awareness!

—YOGA INSTRUCTOR

We are not accustomed to regarding thought and awareness as two different things. Our monkey minds are so busy swinging from thought to thought, chattering so steadily in our brains, that we believe the thought is what we are. For almost four hundred years Western thought has reflected Descartes's powerful dictum: "I think, therefore I am." But Eastern philosophy offers a different paradigm, the concept of Big Mind, of self grounded in a consciousness beyond the thinking brain. Our child may be the one who teaches us that this is so. She may not have language or thoughts as we know them. Yet we know she is there and we have learned the subtle signs through which she communicates.

We have the power to quiet our thoughts, to be still and observe. This is not thinking, but awareness, consciousness, Being.

Focus

Fats, oils and sweets. Use sparingly.

—U.S.D.A. FOOD GUIDE PYRAMID

A father who practiced yoga grew to cherish *shivasana,* or corpse pose, the final pose of relaxation that closed every class. One day, after he had had a quarrel with his daughter's case manager, he found himself rehearsing their exchange during the pose. He did not even hear the teacher's voice instructing him to relax his neck, his arms, his heart. He left class feeling as tense as when he had arrived, and he realized that every time he let his attention focus on someone else instead of on his own body during *shivasana,* he literally gave away those precious, healing minutes.

It is not unusual for us to let others take up residence in our mind, especially when we have strong feelings about our interactions with them. One woman calls this absorption with another "giving Free Air Time," or F.A.T. thinking. In the broadcasting studio of our brains, we turn over the airwaves to someone else. With F.A.T. thinking we give power—power to hurt, to flatter, to antagonize—to the words and actions of others. F.A.T. thinking upsets our peace of mind, diverts our attention from our own goals, and depletes our energy.

Today, I will preserve my focus and serenity by choosing low-fat thinking.

Detachment

If you are in a room with a problem, don't talk to it.

—MICHAEL ONDAATJE

When we have a problem, it can be tempting not just to talk to it but to clutch it to our chest and lavish attention on it. Since we have kids with disabilities, we have plenty of problems to hug and talk to. But problems aren't really very good company. And, ironically, the more attention we pay to them, the more they resist solution. Detaching from the problem can be far more useful. Don't hug it; don't talk to it. Walk out of the room where the problem is staying and shut the door behind you. Once you have put some distance between yourself and the problem, you are more likely to gain perspective and see solutions. Then you can go back in and engage the problem, tell it what action you are going to take, maybe even shake hands with it, but then kiss it goodbye. Make yours the final word.

Risk

From risks I learned. From getting lost I found my way. Finding my way, I learned about my neighborhood and city.

—DAVID DAWSON, A MAN WITH DOWN SYNDROME

When David Dawson says that he found his way from getting lost, he means it literally. It was when he got lost biking around his neighborhood that he finally learned to get around town on his own. But David's words also provide us with a metaphor for the way we all learn. When we try something, we take a risk. We may "get lost" by making mistakes or becoming confused; we may even lose our sense of where we were headed when we started out. Through trial and error we solve the problem, we find our way, we learn.

Whether we are learning a new external task, such as inserting a gastronomy tube, or embarking on an internal effort, such as changing the way we approach problems, it is vital that we take risks even though they may result in our getting lost. David is telling us very explicitly that taking risks and getting lost are not unfortunate elements in a failed effort, but essential steps in learning; that *from* getting lost, we find our way.

The next time I make a mistake or feel lost, I will remember that it is an opportunity to find my way and to learn. The next time I find myself frustrated or angry at others' mistakes, I will remember that they are finding their way.

Anticipation

I skate to where I think the puck will be.

—WAYNE GRETSKY

Live in the moment. Anticipate what's coming. These sound like contradictory injunctions. They might be, if life were static, but it isn't. The present moment is continually unfolding into the next. Our children's development isn't static either, even when change seems slow or impossible. Most of the time, keeping up with their growth and change and needs feels like a game of hockey. We are well advised to keep an eye out for the goal, to anticipate where the puck is going. In life we are always shooting at a moving target. Skate for the flying puck.

Our Spiritual Nature

When I see a baby quietly staring at his or her own hands . . . or a toddler off in a corner putting something into a cup and then taking it out, over and over again . . . or a preschooler lying in the grass daydreaming, I like to think that they, in their own ways, are "alone in the best room" of their houses, using the solitude they need to find the courage to grow.

—FRED ROGERS

We can think of spirituality as the process of finding the "best room" in our inner house and the practice of spending time alone there. We can find our way there through meditation—intense focus on a single object or thought; through repetitive action—reciting familiar prayers, weeding the garden; and through untethering our minds—daydreaming.

In *A Little Book of Forgiveness*, D. Patrick Miller says, "The most effective, *lasting* action arises from profound stillness and radical clarity." We can find that stillness in our "best room." It is there that our thoughts begin to crystallize into diamonds, gems of "radical clarity." In solitude we find the courage to grow, to take the next step. In stillness and clear thinking we discover the path to effective action and lasting change.

The pull to our spiritual self is built into us. Babies and children instinctively go to their best room as they work through the complex task of growing up. But we adults often ignore or override this instinct. We get out of practice and forget the way to our best room; we forget that we have a place to go at all.

Today, let me resume my practice by sitting still for a little while.

Energy

Love is a force. It is not a result; it is a cause. It is not a product; it is power, like money or steam, or electricity.

—ANNE MORROW LINDBERGH

The medieval alchemists believed that there was a way to change base metals, such as lead, into gold. If they could only find the formula! They worked long and hard at it, but the basic hypothesis proved false.

Much of the work attached to raising children is drudgery— dirty, repetitive, boring—and a heavy obligation: we have to do it. Yet we can transmute these mundane chores into activities that give us energy instead of draining it away if we do them not only because we have to, but because we want to. And we will want to do our work, no matter how distasteful in its particulars, when we understand that it is the necessary part of a larger, more meaningful whole to which we have committed ourselves with love.

There is a woman who creates unique and beautiful fabric vessels from knotted silk. It is slow, tedious, meticulous work. Each piece takes at least a year to complete. She must tie thousands of tiny knots. Every day she does the same thing—ties knots—but at the end of each day her work is another step closer to becoming the beautiful object she lovingly imagines. Sustained by that awareness, she returns to her knots each morning with fresh energy.

Knots become a work of art; a series of mundane tasks become the shaping of a human being; the lead of dull duty becomes the gold of energizing love.

The alchemy of the heart is not false.

Death Wish

I must confess something: sometimes I hope Noah gets sick and dies painlessly.

—JOSH GREENFELD, WHOSE SON HAS DEVELOPMENTAL DISABILITIES

You may have never dared utter or admit the thought to another human being, even to your partner, but you are far from alone in having wished your child's peaceful death. You are not the only parent of an infant with a disability who finds himself having dreams or fantasies about his child's death. You are not the only parent who has sat in the hospital emergency room or intensive care unit and thought, "Maybe he'll die." Nor are you the only parent who feels terrible guilt just for having such thoughts, or the only one whose guilt is multiplied because she had those thoughts and her child did die.

Loving our children as we do, we go to extraordinary lengths to help them and care for them. But sometimes death can appear as the only honorable exit, or solution to problems that feel insoluble. Without making painful decisions about medical interventions or placement, and without shame or guilt, we can be free of the dilemma our child's disability presents to our life. Furthermore, our child can be released from real suffering and what we may see as the terrible challenge of her life. Such thoughts are normal when we are faced with difficult choices, none of which seems good. They are normal when we are confronted with extraordinary tasks that seem beyond our capabilities.

Today, I will forgive myself for being human and sometimes wishing my child would die. Today, I will think about how much I love my child and the ways in which I am a good parent to her.

Faith

I hope I outlive her.

—FATHER AT A PARENTS' CONFERENCE, SPEAKING OF HIS
FIVE-YEAR-OLD DAUGHTER, WHO HAS DOWN SYNDROME

Our desire to outlive our children with disabilities is the exact opposite of the typical parental wish to raise a child to adulthood and precede her in death. Under normal circumstances a special sympathy is felt for the parent who loses a child, even when that child is an adult, because it seems a reversal of the natural order of things.

Our wish to survive our child says a lot of things. It says that we want to be there always to take care of her because we know or fear that she can never take care of herself completely. It says that we are afraid to think of her as a ward of the state, totally dependent on institutions and bureaucracy. It says that we hesitate to ask her brothers and sisters to shoulder the responsibility for her care. It says we disbelieve or are unsure that anyone else would love and care for her the way we do, and we are afraid to ask or expect anyone to do so. Buried in our wish is a silent cry: Who will love her as we do?

Let me have faith that someone will care. Let me not decide that we, her parents, are the only ones who can ever love and look out for her. Let me accept that I cannot control this sequence. Whether I am living or not, she must go out into the world as who and what she is. She must ultimately depend, as we all do, on others.

Action

The thing was, I never doubted I would get cured, and the sight of my skinny legs . . . only doubled my determination to "get on with it," as my mother would say. And there was healing euphoria just in that: we were doing something, we were going places.

—WILFRED SHEED, WHOSE LEGS WERE PARALYZED
BY POLIO WHEN HE WAS FOURTEEN

An English couple embarked on a search for a cure when encephalitis, developing out of a case of measles, left their two-year-old daughter, Victoria, unable to talk, walk, or feed herself. At great expense they brought their daughter to Philadelphia and the Institutes for the Achievement of Human Potential, where they studied the "patterning" methods developed by Dr. Glenn Doman. The theory behind patterning is that crawling on the stomach or creeping on hands and knees stimulates the brain cells that govern neurological development. Patterning therapy involves a regimen in which several people simultaneously manipulate the child's body in the desired patterns of movement several times a day for specified periods of time. Its effectiveness remains a matter of controversy.

On their return to England, Victoria's parents began to perform the prescribed exercises with her for five hours every day, a schedule they kept up for years with the help of friends and neighbors. Ultimately, the patterning produced little change in Victoria, but doing something they believed to be positive for their child relieved her parents' feelings of helplessness and rage. For Victoria's mother, the realization that she could search out and implement her own solutions gave her a new sense of control over her life. And when the patterning failed, she was able to focus on what

Victoria needed most if she was never going to walk or talk. Seeing how isolated her daughter was, she set out to bring children into Victoria's life and eventually founded the first inclusive nursery school in her city.

Searching for a cure can sometimes seem the only alternative to feeling helpless, hopeless, and tragic. Sometimes it is part of our "bargaining with God" stage: "I'll scour the earth for the cure, God, if you will just provide it." Other times, what may appear to be a search for a cure is no more than our conscientious effort to uncover any treatment or intervention that might help our child; no more than our need to take some kind of action.

Even when we have accepted the reality of our child's disability and dismissed the idea of a cure, the healthy impulse to fight back leads us to action and to the more immediate ways we can respond to our child, which include loving and teaching her at home and working to make a place for her in the community. As long as we have a course of action, something we believe is useful to do, we can go forward.

Supermom

If a perfect parent is not what a child needs, what is? A mother who is, in the words of child psychologist D. W. Winnicott, "good enough."

—BRIE P. QUINBY

Amanda tells the story of the first year she took her two-year-old son to early-childhood classes. Each Tuesday at class the specialists would teach the mothers new exercises and activities to encourage their toddlers' delayed development. In the ensuing week Amanda would work with Peter at home, diligently adding that week's new activities to the ones she had already learned. Soon she felt she was doing therapy all day long. When she failed to get through everything—which was often, since she had two little girls who also needed her attention—she felt terribly guilty.

One day in class she burst into tears. "I just can't do all of this," she sobbed. "I know Peter really needs this, but it's taking all day!" "You're not trying to do all the exercises every day are you?" asked one of the teachers. "Well, isn't that what we're supposed to do?" answered the distraught Amanda. The teacher quickly explained that parents were taught a variety of activities for all aspects of their child's growth, with the idea that they would concentrate on a few at a time. "Only do what you reasonably can," she said. "Anything you do will help Peter."

Amanda felt she could never do enough for her child. She also worried that if she didn't do everything and do it just right, she would harm Peter or somehow compromise his development. Her guilt and anxiety had clouded her judgment and distorted her thinking.

There is a sense in which no parent of any child can ever do enough. We are limited human beings who can do only our best each day. While parents definitely can harm a child through aggressive action or neglect, the opposite of harm and neglect is not total, perfect care. Our children are strong and resilient. It is possible to be good enough for each of them, whatever his needs.

Bad Luck

Some people, lightning struck twice. Some people attracted accidents. Fate bunched up and gathered like a blanket. Some people were born on the smooth parts and some got folded into the pucker.

—LOUISE ERDRICH, WHOSE ADOPTED SON
HAD FETAL ALCOHOL SYNDROME

Some of us surely must feel that we live in the pucker of fate. Due to what was hidden in our genes, or perhaps because of mere coincidence, we have two or even three children with disabilities. Others of us have been stricken by other catastrophic events or extraordinary hardships in addition to having a child with a disability. Or we have stretches when difficulties and "bad luck" pile up on us. Where is the fairness in this? In the scheme of things as far as we understand it, fairness is beside the point. Some people's lives are harder than other people's. It's just so. It doesn't make us failures or losers, although we may feel we have failed or lost out in some essential way. In reality, we didn't do anything to "deserve" to be "born in the pucker." These are our life circumstances.

Today, let me have the strength to live my life where it is and as it is.

Growing Up

Thank you for letting me grow up.

—MATT CARRATURO, A YOUNG MAN WITH DOWN SYNDROME

Letting our child grow up is a constant challenge for parents. Is it time to start solid foods? Can we leave him with a sitter? Is she old enough to go home with a friend after school? Should I let her cross the street by herself? She wants to pierce her ears! He wants to go on vacation with his friend's family, take the car, ride his bike across the state! The struggle is between our responsibility and concern for the child's safety, and his need to take risks and have experiences that will help him develop the skills and competence to live without us.

As with so many parenting issues, this one is more complicated when it is about our child with a disability. We know she has greater vulnerability, and we have fewer models or guidelines to follow. "What are the other kids doing?" doesn't get us very far. We feel more susceptible to having our judgment questioned or challenged. What may seem reasonable to us—perhaps letting our child go one block to the small neighborhood park—looks to our neighbor like a matter for county child protection.

We are afraid when we watch our sixteen-year-old drive off alone in the car for the first time. We let him do it, even though the risk is huge: he may make mistakes that could cost him his life. Nevertheless, our society considers this a reasonable and necessary risk. Similarly, we are afraid when our sixteen-year-old with a cognitive disability takes the bus alone. Here too there is a risk of injury and even death. Just as we take risks with our "normal" child, we must take reasonable risks with our child with a disability, even though our heart is in our throat.

Our own fear or uncertainty may be causing us to underestimate our child's capabilities. We may have bought in to the idea that protection is more important than learning, and that our child's safety can be guaranteed. These ideas cause us to avoid taking risks or permitting our child—whether still small or an adult—from taking necessary risks. In fact, our challenge is to balance protection and risk, and to remember that risk is essential to learning and is a part of life for everyone.

Give me the wisdom and courage to let my child do the things and take the risks that will enable her to grow up to be the most competent person she can be.

Control

Experience is the best teacher.

—OLD SAYING

A mother tried to do everything just right for her special child. She was always anticipating situations where he couldn't, or didn't, express his needs and making sure he was taken care of. Once he started school, she worried even more. This was not a child who could call to say he forgot his lunch. And she did not want the teachers to think she was careless or neglectful.

One mild winter day as the school bus pulled away she saw his mittens lying on the floor, forgotten. Immediately this supermom felt panic and stress wash over her. "Damn! He's forgotten his mittens! If I hurry, I can drop them off on my way to work." As she pulled on her coat and rushed to the garage, the precious mittens in hand, she stopped cold. Pictures of herself as a child flashed into her mind. There she was on the school playground on a winter's day, bare hands in her pockets; or trudging home from sledding, soaking wet mittens dangling, useless, from their clips. "What," she thought, "if he grew up and left home and had never once been out in the cold without his mittens?"

In that moment she saw that her job was not to prevent and solve all the problems that arose for her child, but to give him the opportunity to experience those problems and solve them himself. Even if she could manage and control every aspect of his life, to do so would be to fail herself and him.

Starting Point

Keep your eye on the ball.

—SPORTS SLOGAN

We moms and dads work extremely hard. We are whirlwinds of busyness—planning, "implementing," and "advocating." We listen a lot to the opinions and advice of others—our spouse, the doctor, the teacher, other parents—and become absorbed with meeting our kid's daily demands and needs. Sometimes we forget that it is our child who is at the center of all this activity and energy. Totally engaged in fulfilling *our* idea of how things should be for him, we neglect to ask him what his idea is. Occupied with trying to figure out what is what, we forget to sit still and learn what we can from simple observation.

This lesson was brought home forcefully to a mother who had chosen a mainstream classroom for her ten-year-old son with attention deficit disorder. When a learning-disabilities advocate urged her to move the child to a special classroom because it would be better for his self-esteem, the mother agonized over the advice, weighing and reweighing the pros and cons. Finally she asked her son what he thought about being mainstreamed. "Mom," he replied, "I am the mainstream."

Maybe understanding our child means asking him and really listening to what he says. Maybe it means being attentive to the words behind the words. Maybe it means noticing that when there is music playing, he smiles more; or that when he's involved with other kids, he withdraws less. So often the answer is not at the end of an expanding spiral of activity and inquiry, but at its beginning, in the center, where our child is.

Voice

It was not hard to talk to Adam, even though I didn't know if he could hear me. I had put words in his mouth so often over the years that the process came naturally. I supplied the questions, and I provided the right answers.

—MICHAEL DORRIS, WHOSE SON ABEL HAD FETAL ALCOHOL SYNDROME. (IN HIS BOOK ABOUT ABEL, DORRIS CALLS HIM ADAM.)

When Janet's parents decided to go ahead with the permanent tracheotomy that permits her to breathe on her own, they had to trade off her ability to speak. Now Janet communicates with a kind of signing called finger spelling. Recently Janet became angry with her mother because she wanted to go to the library and her mother hadn't made clear whether they would go or when. Janet spelled her message to her mother. The angrier she became, the faster her fingers flew. Her face was red and scrunched. Because her mother knows from her facial expression when Janet is angry, she raises her voice as she articulates Janet's signing: "W-h-e-n When, a-r-e are, w-e we, g-o-i-n-g going!" Then, because she is angry, too, her mother shouts her own responses.

Later, thinking about the scene, the mother doesn't know whether to laugh or cry. It's bad enough when your kids yell at you, but when you have to yell at yourself for them it borders on the ridiculous. She knows that she could have articulated Janet's signing in a speaking voice. But even though she has the power to do so, she would not dream of denying her daughter an angry voice.

We ask the questions and supply the answers. We shout at ourselves and shout back. We translate our children's garbled speech

130

for others. It is a lot of physical, mental, and emotional work to be someone else's voice. It is also a sacred responsibility.

Today, even if I am the one providing the sound or even the words, I will strive to let my child make her own statements, ask her own questions, give her own answers. Today, let me be only the channel for the river of her thoughts and intentions.

Just in Case

Yet these tiny successes accomplished something. Narrow as Elly's spectrum remained, it was less narrow than before. Each minuscule, apparently empty victory nourished something in Elly and in us.

—CLARA CLAIBORNE PARK

She has never called your name or said Daddy.
You don't know whether she understands what you say.
She seems to see, but you are not sure she recognizes you.
Once, months and months ago, she handed you a toy.
Occasionally, perhaps when she is placed in a warm bath, or when
there is butter on her food, you see a smile.
When you play music, she stops crying.
Every few months she says a word.
Nourished on these crumbs, you keep on holding, stroking, bath-
ing, feeding, smiling, and talking, talking, talking. Just in case
she can hear, just in case she does understand, just in case she
does know.

Change Syndrome

JASON: *Down syndrome will change to "up" syndrome, and that will make Down syndrome go away.*

MITCHELL: *No, the disability never can change. We'll call it "change" syndrome. Things change around if you think about it. The reason we should call it "change" syndrome is we can't change the disability, but we can change the way we feel.*

—JASON KINGSLEY AND MITCHELL LEVITZ, TWO YOUNG MEN
WHO HAVE DOWN SYNDROME

Our child's disability is real. We can't change it or wish it away. We don't want to live in delusion, and even if we did, the reality of our child's needs won't let us. We can't get rid of the "down," but we can cultivate the habit of seeing and attending to the "up." And the truth is that we can literally change our perceptions and our feelings about our child's disability—about anything, for that matter—by the way we think and talk about it. That is not denying reality or trying to compensate for a bad situation. It is a healthy awareness that our mind plays a significant part in shaping our reality, and that life will be better when we work with what we've got, instead of lamenting what we're missing.

You've got change syndrome when you watch your kid walking on his crutches and all you see is that he's walking. You'll recognize its effects the day you hear your son telling his little brother about the times he's been teased at school and what he did about it, and what gets your attention is not that your learning disabled son was teased, but that here is a situation in which he can really be the big brother, using his own experience to guide the younger one through problems. It's definitely change syndrome when you find your child sitting fully clothed in a bathtub of water and you are thrilled because he understood what you meant when you said it was time for his bath.

Gratitude

You do not notice changes in what is always before you.

—COLETTE

We respond to a problem with our child the same way we do to undesirable weather: obsess about it while it persists and forget about it as soon as it goes away. Just as quickly as complaints about the excessively rainy summer gave way to concern about this winter's storms, our attention shifts from the head banging we struggled with for three years to the dental problems that have since surfaced. Out of sight is out of mind.

Sometimes the new problem takes over so smoothly that we aren't even aware that the old one has gone away, until one day we look up and say, "My God, it's been weeks since Jason woke up at night!" We have just plunged into the next issue without pausing to mark the disappearance of the one that was troubling us so much. In any familiar situation or relationship it is important to step back occasionally and try to see it as if for the first time. In any journey it is important to measure not only how far you have left to go—something it may be impossible to know—but how far you have already come.

Today, I will take time to think over the past week, month, or year and note the progress we and our child have made, count the problems that were solved, remember all the things that were driving us to distraction six months ago and are now gone. Today, I'll have a little party for the stuff that went away!

Sense of Self

We name ourselves by the choices we make . . . To name is to love.
To be Named is to be loved.

—MADELEINE L'ENGLE

Choices, self-naming, and self-love are the doorways to identity,
one leading into the next. To deny or interfere excessively with an
individual's exercise of choice is to impair his growth and development, and to encourage what is known as "learned helplessness."

As parents we automatically make scores of choices for our children every day, from what they're going to eat to how they will
spend their time. It's easy for us to slip into making all the choices,
and to get in the habit of scrutinizing and questioning the choices
our children make. Even though our choices may be "better"—yes,
fruit is a better snack than candy—what is more important is that
our child have the opportunity to make her own choices, good and
bad.

People of all ages with exceptional dependencies are constantly
having the right to choose taken from them, and thus being denied
or stripped of a piece of their identity and their sense of competence. We need vigilantly to guard our child's right to make choices
in the world at large as well as at home.

I will let my child choose what to be and what to do, knowing
that this freedom is essential to her growth and identity.

Reservoir

The majority of people perform well in a crisis and when the spotlight is on them; it's on the Sunday afternoons of this life, when nobody is looking, that the spirit falters.

—ALAN BENNETT

Crises present situations in which we perform well because the choices are clear-cut and the need to act is compelling. When our daughter has a seizure or a 105 degree fever or an asthma attack, we know what to do. Our adrenaline kicks in and we move swiftly and decisively to respond. Although a crisis exacts a toll, in the moment it is a snap. "It is easy," says Louise Erdrich, describing one of her son's seizures, "to be the occasional ministering angel. But it is not easy to live day in and day out with a child disabled by fetal alcohol syndrome."

The days in and the days out. Those Sunday afternoons offstage when nobody is looking. These are not easy. It is there and then that our spirit falters. It is for these moments that we build an inner reservoir, ready to be tapped for the subtle crises of the soul.

Build from Strength

The other teachers and professionals at the school wanted to discourage my weird interests and make me more normal, but Mr. Carlock took my interests and used them as motivators for doing schoolwork.

—TEMPLE GRANDIN, WHO HAS AUTISM

A couple were frustrated with the way their daughter's mainstream teacher constantly focused on what she couldn't do or how she misbehaved. They tried to convey to the teacher that the difficulties their daughter had in learning and managing her behavior were part of her disability. They urged him to deal with her on her terms, to work from her strengths, and to remember that her failings were not willful or the result of lack of discipline at home.

However, as the year wore on it dawned on them that they were treating the teacher the same way he was treating their daughter. They were never satisfied with him and had nothing but complaints. They were asking him to stretch—to teach a child whose ways of learning were new to him—yet, by being constantly critical, they were emphasizing his lacks and weaknesses. His attitudes and inflexibility were *his* disabilities, they realized.

We communicate people's strengths to them through praise. We encourage the baby in the difficult task of walking by clapping and cheering and saying, "You can do it!" even though she's tottering at every step. All of us have to extend ourselves to develop new skills or do new things, but we must begin with abilities we already have, and we must receive encouragement even for shaky steps.

For teachers and students, parents and children—for all of us—strengths are the only place to begin.

Surrender

What true spiritual leaders are asking of us in the concept of acceptance and surrender is one thing only: to accept our unity with all life, and surrender our fantasy of separation.

—CHRISTINA BALDWIN

Rappelling is the technique mountain climbers use to descend cliffs or slopes too difficult to climb down. In rappelling, the climber doubles his rope by anchoring it around a tree or rock at the top of the cliff. Looping one end of the rope around his shoulder and leg so as to make a sort of pulley of his own body, the climber then plants his feet on the cliff wall and begins to pay out the rope, using one hand as a brake to control the speed of descent as he backs down the rock face. The trick is this: to move, the climber has to let the rope move through his hands. In a sense he has to hang on and let go at the same time. When you are hanging in midair with your back perpendicular to the ground, unable to see where you are going, it's hard to let go. Your instinct is to grip the rope or, as climbers say, "white knuckle."

Many of the situations we encounter when raising a child with a disability can feel a lot like rappelling. We're hanging in air; we can't see where we are going; we're scared. It is difficult to trust Whoever is anchoring the rope. But if we don't let go—if we "white knuckle" and the rope cannot slide through our hands— we're stuck. We cannot get to the bottom of whatever cliff we have to descend. We must give up the idea that we are acting alone, and accept that there are greater powers at work in the universe.

Today, I will relax my grip on the rope and trust that I will not fall.

Breathing

Breathe in, and as you do think of your body filling with light. As you exhale, the light intensifies.

—YOGA INSTRUCTOR

Lie flat on your back on the floor with your legs spread wider than your hips. Turn your shoulders out so that the insides of your arms and your palms face the ceiling. Close your eyes. Consciously relax your body, letting it sink into the floor. Pay attention to your belly. Watch the breath there; as you inhale, your belly rises; as you exhale, it falls. Don't force it; just observe it. If your thoughts wander, bring them back to the breath. On an inhalation, move your attention to the breath in your nostrils. Watch the breath going in and out. Imagine that each inhalation is bringing light to every cell of your body. Imagine that each exhalation is expelling anything toxic, carrying away disease or dark emotion. Don't fret if your attention wanders. Just come back, come back to your breath. Breathing and paying attention to your breath can bring you calm and peace. Imagine your breath filling every cell, carrying your awareness to every part of your body; let it restore and renew you. Spirit comes from the Latin *spiritus*, which means breath. As we observe our inspirations and expirations coming and going with no effort on our part, we understand that our breath, which is our very life, is a gift.

Inviolate Core

Innocent When You Dream

—TITLE OF A SONG BY TOM WAITS

The film *The Shawshank Redemption* tells the story of a man serving a life sentence in a corrupt and brutal prison for a crime he didn't commit. One day, in his role as prison librarian, he receives a shipment of books and records. He slips into the prison office, locks the door, and plays a Mozart aria over the prison public address system. For this offense he is put in solitary confinement for a month. When he is released, he tells his friends that hearing the music was worth the confinement, because the music lives on in his mind and cannot be taken from him by the guards. That is what hope is, he says: that part of yourself they can't ever get to.

The wider the gap between our inner reality and the realities being imposed upon us—be they patronizing attitudes about disability, or the Byzantine world of the social service bureaucracy—the more important it is that we maintain our core and let it guide us. This is the touchstone for our sense of reality, the seedbed of our hopes and dreams. We all need to find and nourish that space in ourselves that no one can get to, our inviolate core.

Stepparent

The last time Spencer came back from visiting his dad I sent flowers to Connie, because I know she's the one who looks after him when he's there and I am so grateful that she cares for him.

—JACQUELINE, WHOSE ADULT SON HAS DOWN SYNDROME, SPEAKING OF HIS VISITS TO HIS FATHER AND STEPMOTHER

Not all the stepmothers and stepfathers are wicked. A lot of us are like Connie. When we married the guy, we accepted all his kids, including the one with a disability. We went in with our eyes open. If we didn't know it already, we quickly learned that parenting is difficult under the best of circumstances, and that it can be really tough to love and parent kids who aren't yours. But we also learned that our outsider status brings with it some objectivity and distance that can be a gift to the parent and the child.

If we are lucky, the child's other parent recognizes and appreciates what we do. But if they don't, so what? After all, we did not make this commitment in order to win the approval of our spouse's ex. We made it because we love our partner. Whether our sacrifices and contributions are acknowledged or not, we have the satisfaction of knowing we did the right thing for a child.

Siblings

Every brother is a dork sometimes, even if he has a disability.

—ROB, AGE SIX, WHOSE OLDER BROTHER IS DEAF

John, a nine-year-old boy, is asked to describe life with his brother Brad, twelve, who has Down syndrome. "Sometimes good and sometimes horrible," he says. "It is good because I can con him easily. Sometimes he shares his toys, and sometimes he's understanding." Then he goes on to enumerate a much longer list of the horrible things: "He screams when I take something of his. He's not a good sport at games sometimes. He gets up early in the morning and hogs the leftover pizza so no one else can get it. We go to the same school, and people always come up to me and say Brad did this or Brad did that. I'm having a great time and they come up to me and say are you Brad's brother. I tell them to work it out themselves. I'm way better at Nintendo than he is."

How much simpler life would be if your big brother were just a dork. How confusing for a child to have to figure out what is dorkiness and what behavior is the result of the disability. How troubling to be asked to be responsible for your big brother, or to mediate the issues between him and other schoolmates. How hard to be the little brother and be "way better."

We don't need to deny the horrible side, or try to talk our child out of his anger or embarrassment. We just need to tell him we hear him, and though we try to understand, we don't know exactly what it's like to have a brother who is different from the other kids. We do know there are a lot of hard parts, and we are there to help him through them. We can tell him we know he loves his brother even when he hates him, and that we love them both, more than anything. And, yes, sometimes a brother is just a dork, plain and simple.

Jargon

They had a special language: regression, acting out, hostility, withdrawal, indulging in behavior. *This last phrase could be attached to any activity and make it sound suspicious: indulging in eating behavior, talking behavior, writing behavior. In the outside world people ate and talked and wrote, but nothing we did was simple.*

—SUSANNA KAYSEN

Other parents play with their babies; we do learning programs.

Other kids have brothers and sisters; ours has sibling relationships.

Other teenagers have a job; ours is in competitive employment.

Other babies start to talk; ours is developing her expressive language.

Other families have a baby sitter; we have a PCA—personal care attendant.

Other kids go to school; ours receives services.

Other kids play and exercise; ours has therapies.

Other kids get in trouble at school; ours has a behavioral incident.

Other kids leave home; ours transitions out.

Other people speak plain English; I will insist on it, too.

Losing It

The lid blows off. Nothing is left. If I can't help him to survive in the simplest way, how can I be his mother?

—LOUISE ERDRICH

Louise Erdrich describes trying to get her adopted son, who has fetal alcohol syndrome (FAS), to eat, because if he doesn't he will have a seizure. Dinner is long over, but he is still sitting at the table, staring at his untouched food. Louise has been through her repertoire: Patient urging. Offering choices. A compromise. Ordering. Begging. Pleading. It's eight o'clock at night. Her husband is away on a trip. She has three little children who need to be put to bed. Finally, she snaps: "Don't eat then. And don't call me Mom!"

We have all been brought to the bottom, probably many times. Maybe even today. We've tried every tool in our box. We've exercised more patience than we ever knew we had. And it's still not enough. We run out. We blow up. We have a tantrum. We scream and stomp. Maybe we hit. Maybe, like Louise, we give up entirely. One mother says that she now realizes that violent anger comes not from a need to show power, but from a feeling of almost total helplessness and loss of control.

If I have lost it today, I will acknowledge that fact. First, I will forgive myself. Then, I will apologize to my child and my family. Finally, I will remember that tomorrow is a new day and I can begin again.

Capacity

We are all asked to do more than we can do.

—MADELEINE L'ENGLE

There is a popular saying to the effect that God never gives us more than we can handle. Perhaps people have said this to you in their effort to comfort you or shore you up. And perhaps when they said it you did not feel comforted to think that you had been hand-picked for a task that felt unfair and overwhelming. Perhaps you did not feel at all qualified or capable of carrying the load.

All the best stories, from Moses to *Little Women* to Rocky, are about people who were not qualified, who were given more than they could handle, and somehow overcame their limitations. We love these stories because they affirm that we all have the capacity as human beings to enlarge ourselves, to grow in response to life's challenges.

Rain

That's too bad, it's raining.

—SAM DASHNER, A MAN WITH AUTISM

In *No Pity*, a chronicle of the disability rights movement, Joseph Shapiro tells the story of Sam Dashner, a man with autism whose biggest barrier to getting a job was a pathological fear of the rain. Sam was able to hold down a job successfully after a psychologist taught him to check the weather report, carry an umbrella and raincoat when there was any chance of rain, and to respond to rain by saying to himself, over and over, "That's too bad; it's raining."

We all have to learn a version of Sam's lesson, because we all respond to certain realities in ways that disturb or upset us and thus stand in our way. We may be telling ourselves such things as "My life is ruined because of this child's disability," or "I cannot work with this health aide because I don't like him." We may be letting whole days be marred because our daughter's group home director calls frequently to complain about her, or because when we went to school we saw that our child's desk was alone at the back of the room and all the other children were seated in groups.

Rain falls into every life, and more falls into some. Nevertheless, it is still just rain. Like Sam, we need to learn and practice a new response to the things that frighten us and make us anxious. We need to say, "It's raining; that's too bad," grab our umbrella, and get to work.

Problems

One of the many advantages of seeing Things As They Are is that we can solve problems through observation and deduction. After all, how can we solve problems if we can't first clearly see what they are?

—BENJAMIN HOFF

We tend to think of a problem as something negative. "What's the problem?" and "What's wrong?" are practically interchangeable questions. Many problems are in fact negative or come to our attention because something has broken or gone wrong. But at base a problem is just something to solve. It is a situation that presents a question.

As the *Te of Piglet* advises, "[I]n solving problems, one needs to know if they *are* problems. Is what appears at first to be bad *truly* bad?" Unfortunately, we sometimes ignore certain situations, or fret in a state of inaction, because we don't want to deal with something bad. If we thought of it instead as something that needed to be figured out, we might not put so much energy into avoiding it.

Other times, having acknowledged that there is a problem, we jump to solutions and conclusions before we are clear about what the question is or how the problem could be defined. If many people are gathered around the problem, they may put forward conflicting solutions. Soon individuals are defending their solutions when the group hasn't even agreed on what the problem is. As an individual, as part of a couple, or as a member of a team, the parent of a child with a disability is called on to respond to many questions, many problems, regarding his child.

Today, I will remember to keep asking: Is there a problem? What is it? What is the question? What is the state of Things as They Are?

Stop

Now, here you see, it takes all the running you can do, to keep in the same place. If you want to get somewhere else, you must run at least twice as fast as that!

—LEWIS CARROLL

Do I find myself stressed, tense, overwhelmed, and pissed off? When I feel this way, is my impulse to make my behavior more intense, do more, push harder, talk louder? Am I afraid that if I stop, I won't be able to start again?

This behavior pattern is an occupational hazard for us whose child has a disability. We need an inner early warning system that alerts us when we are heading down this path. As the Supremes used to sing "Stop! In the name of love." In the name of loving ourselves, we must avoid operating on overload.

Am I strung out, tearful, overextended, and perturbed? The warning is contained in an acronym of the symptoms: S-T-O-P. The harder it is for us to stop, the more we need to pay attention, because what seems impossible—stopping—is the one thing we most need to do. If we ignore the symptoms and persist in doing more, we will literally collapse, becoming physically ill or severely, even clinically, depressed.

Today, I will remember to S-T-O-P when I find myself feeling Stretched, Trapped, Overtired, Pressured.

Conscious Repose

There is no effort in this pose, only letting go. Concentrate as much on letting go as you do on exerting yourself.

—YOGA INSTRUCTOR

Can you remember the last day you lived without a list of things to do? Or the last time no one was depending on you for anything? When did you spend a whole day without knowing what time it was? Or doing exactly what you wanted without talking to yourself about "should" and "ought"?

The ability to relax and step out of time is an essential skill, and like any skill, it must be exercised. That's why yoga students practice the passive crocodile and corpse poses, as well as the warrior stance, which demands strength and effort. In both kinds of poses they practice being alert and focused. Unless we assume a position of conscious repose, we collapse like an overstretched rubber band when we stop our activities. Crashing with exhaustion does not renew us in the way that choosing to take time off—being off from time—does. The poses of ambition, action, and accomplishment are necessary and important, but rest, relaxation, and renewal have their own poses.

Today, to free myself from the clock, I will practice a relaxing pose with my full attention.

Responsibility

Nothing strengthens the judgment and quickens the conscience like individual responsibility.

—ELIZABETH CADY STANTON

A couple who had just moved to a new city joined a support group for parents of children with autism. At the first meeting they told an unhappy story of their difficulty in getting their child properly diagnosed, largely because of the failings of their pediatrician, who had dismissed their persistent expressions of concern, delayed referring the child for assessment, and then, following assessment, avoided giving them a clear diagnosis. After eighteen frustrating months, the parents had found a new pediatrician, who told them plainly that their son was autistic. Their child was now seven years old, but as they recounted their experience, the indignation in their voices was as fresh as if it had happened yesterday. Many of their listeners nodded and murmured assent, acknowledging a familiar tale.

Then one woman said, "Clearly, what your first doctor did was inappropriate, but if you were unhappy with her from the beginning, why did you stay with her? Why didn't you get a new doctor right away?" The couple was stunned. They had never considered how they had contributed to the situation.

Too often our part is failing to assume responsibility for and control over our lives. We stay with a doctor or a home health aide with whom we are not satisfied, or persist with a bad classroom situation or unacceptable group home, not identifying and exercising the choices we do have.

Today, if I am having a problem regarding my child's care or education, I will ask myself whether I am satisfied. If the answer is no, I will sit down and make a list of every possible solution I can think of, no matter how farfetched or improbable. Then I will determine what I can do to solve the problem.

Double Bind

Part of the problem was that being paralyzed was such a good rationalization for feeling miserable that people, no matter what their profession, could see no way out, and could only commiserate. I desperately wanted something better, but could not see how to go about it. Neither could the people whom I had hired to help me; they were incapacitated by my disability, just as I was.

—ARNOLD BEISSER

Arnold Beisser, whose legs were paralyzed by polio in 1950, just as he was beginning his medical career, sought counseling and psychiatric assistance in coming to grips with his condition. But, as he writes, the people he hoped could help him were professionally incapacitated by their perceptions of disability.

Each of us has encountered some version of this double bind at one time or another. We know our child has a poor bite, but when he reaches the age for braces, our dentist doesn't suggest them. He assumes that our child's cognitive handicap precludes his participation in orthodontic treatment. The therapist we are seeing overlooks our depression because she thinks deep, persistent sadness is an inescapable part of having a child with a handicap. The people we seek help from, or look up to as trained authorities, whether pediatricians, ministers, or therapists, have attitudes or emotional responses to disability that interfere with their ability to help us. We find out that when it comes to disability, we have to help them.

I will seek out professionals who have experience with disability and are not impaired in their ability to give me the help I am seeking. I will find professionals who are willing to listen and learn.

Managing

It's up to you to coordinate and monitor the many elements that have to work together for your child to get the services he needs. It's a time-consuming task, and some parents find it helpful to think of it as their "job."

—ROBIN SIMONS

Getting our kids' needs met is an incredible amount of work. We find ourselves thrust into myriad new roles—advocate, case manager, medical coordinator, supervisor. It is easily a full-time job, but few of us have the luxury to approach it that way. We need to keep our paying job, and we have a household to run and other children to take care of. It is really mind-boggling, and to most of us infuriating, that the service and parent advocacy systems, which are supposed to help us, are organized on the assumption and expectation that we can and will assume this added work. The long-term solution is the sensible reform of the systems so that parents don't have to work so hard to get help. Nevertheless, in the short term, most of us will continue to do the extra work, juggling things as best we can so that our child has what she needs.

One dad maintains his sense of humor about this situation by keeping in mind two acronyms from his military experience. One, the GIs brought back from World War II: SNAFU—Situation Normal: All Fouled Up; the other, he learned from his tactics instructors—KISS—Keep It Simple, Stupid. In the face of the expanded chores and responsibilities he and his wife face as parents of a child with a disability, he has enlarged the KISS principle to what he calls KIS KIM KIS KIP: Keep It Simple. Keep It Moving. Keep It Short. Keep It in Perspective. It keeps him sane.

Doctors

I have become a wary consumer of medical services. Never again will I take what a doctor says at face value; I believe in second, and even third opinions.

—MARY PIELAET, WHOSE SON, JON, HAS CEREBRAL PALSY

There is a great scene in the movie *Mask* when Rusty Dennis confronts the new doctor who has said that her son Rocky has three to six months to live. Rusty explodes in the man's face, telling him that she's been listening to doctors for twelve years—doctors saying Rocky was retarded, that he will be blind and deaf, that there is no way he can live a normal life. She concludes by saying that if she had dug her son's grave every time a doctor told her Rocky was going to die, she'd be in China by now. The new doctor was partially right: Rocky did die from the excessive pressure his expanding cranium put on his spinal cord. But he died at sixteen, not at thirteen. He had three more years to live, not three months. The other doctors had been wrong, too. Rocky was not retarded, blind, or deaf, but extremely bright and articulate, keenly alive to life's pleasures as well as to the unique pain it held for him because cranio-diafacial dysplasia had enlarged and distorted his face, making it look as if he wore a lion mask.

Wouldn't we all love to deliver a speech like Rusty's just once! Haven't we all at one time or another believed the professional who felt compelled to predict the future, complete with details? Who thought it was her job to state statistical probabilities, or even mere possibilities, as certain fact? Who made a prognosis out of a diagnosis? Haven't we all sat up nights, worrying and waiting for the pneumonia that never came? Or watched in vindication as our child *did* learn to read? Haven't we all dug our child's grave in one way or another because we mistakenly placed absolute faith in what a doctor said?

Doctors are human beings who have some information or knowledge that will help our children. Some are very skilled, and many are average. They have strengths and weaknesses. They make mistakes in their work. If we don't put them on pedestals, we won't have to knock them off later.

School

Dare you see a Soul at the White Heat?
Then crouch within the door—

—EMILY DICKINSON

Here is what a few mothers have said about their experiences when trying to secure an appropriate education for their child.
INGA: *I felt I was going crazy. Only once before in my life had I felt so low, and that was the year my mother died.* SHERELL: *I was constantly depressed. I gained twenty pounds; I couldn't focus on anything.* JEANETTE: *For the entire year after they threatened me, I did not go to school unless I absolutely had to, even for concerts or programs. Every time I walked in the door, my eyes would fill with tears.* ANDREA: *In order to avoid doing what we wanted, they attacked us at the meeting. I was completely unprepared and totally humiliated. Even now when I think about it I feel ashamed and enraged.* TONI: *I feel the teachers and I are rivals instead of partners. The message I get is that they know what's best for Tom, and that I am not doing everything I should be doing for him.* BRENDA: *My experiences as a teacher led my husband and me to adopt two boys with disabilities. The only times I've regretted doing it have been in relation to school—the years when things were horrible at school.*

These women are describing anguish, suffering, and despair at the deepest level. They are not an isolated, unstable few who cannot work with other people or solve problems effectively. They are diverse in their backgrounds and education, and what they say is representative of the experience that mothers have with school systems. Something is clearly very wrong.

Today, if I am involved in a struggle at school, I will know that I am not alone and I am not the problem. I will recognize that I am engaged in a real battle in which my child's future and my mental health are at stake. I will get help. When I go where my risk of injury is high, I will protect myself in order to protect my child.

Political Fear

The only thing we have to fear is fear itself.

—FRANKLIN D. ROOSEVELT, THIRTY-SECOND PRESIDENT OF THE
UNITED STATES, WHOSE LEGS WERE PARALYZED
BY POLIO WHEN HE WAS THIRTY-NINE

If you have a child with a disability, sometimes just picking up the morning paper can be a terrifying exercise. Right there on the front page, under an inflammatory headline, is an article on how special education is getting too expensive and "takes away" from the education of "normal" children. The lives of children and adults with disabilities have always been subject to law and politics. We pay attention to those facts because few of us have the resources or live in the kind of community that enables us to meet our child's needs and our family's needs without using public schools, social service programs, or subsidized medical programs. And it has taken nothing less than Supreme Court cases and federal legislation to secure basic civil rights for persons with disabilities.

When we see a threat to the tenuous position in society of persons with disabilities, when the public tone turns ugly, we become frightened, even terrified. Not only may we lose a benefit that is crucial to our child, but it seems that our neighbors may be viewing us as enemies.

Fear is poisonous and paralyzing. I will not give in to fear. I will remain calm and clear-eyed. I will decide whether or not to get involved in the political fray. I will determine what is the most important, effective action for me today.

Mantra

It's important to have a vision. Without a vision, people perish.

—ERNESTO J. CORTES

A woman who is a veteran advocate, and the mother of an adult daughter with developmental disabilities, uses the phrase "The sky is blue" as a mantra. Whenever she is going to meet a person from whom she needs something, whether she is representing her daughter or someone else, she keeps those words uppermost in her mind. " 'The sky is blue' stands for what I want, what I'm seeking. Whenever the group home director or the principal or the county case worker—or whoever I'm dealing with—says why we can't do the thing I'm asking, I repeat to myself, 'The sky is blue.' I play that phrase like a broken record in my head. The sky is blue. The sky is blue. The sky is blue."

A mantra is like a code that keeps us focused on what we want and prevents us from getting diverted by irrelevant issues. "The sky is blue" reminds us that anything is possible. It helps us keep our eye on the horizon, the big picture, our vision. It keeps us positive. It may be raining today, but we know that beyond the clouds the sky is blue.

Political Correctness

Mr. and Mrs. Little often discussed Stuart quietly between themselves when he wasn't around, for they had never quite recovered from the shock and surprise of having a mouse in the family. He was so very tiny and he presented so many problems to his parents. Mr. Little said that, for one thing, there must be no references to "mice" in their conversation. He made Mrs. Little tear from the nursery songbook the page about "Three Blind Mice, See How They Run."

—E. B. WHITE

A mother who often spoke of her son as "my handicapped child" found herself apologizing for that phrase when she got up to talk at a parent-training session where much emphasis had been placed on politically correct, "people first" language: "people with developmental disabilities," "a person with a seizure disorder," "my son who is visually impaired."

This mother's dilemma was particularly acute, because her son had all of those handicapping conditions plus others. She understood the points she had learned in the workshops—that the labels attached to a person with handicaps can get in the way of that individual being perceived first and last as a person; that how we talk about people can shape how we think about them and how we treat them; that the language used about those with handicaps does in fact tend to objectify them and to reflect society's prejudicial attitudes toward them.

But this mother also understood that when she was chatting with another parent at her older daughter's soccer game and volunteered that she had a son "with severe and profound multiple handicaps," the other person didn't really know what she was talking about. She knew that when she said, "I have a son with developmental disabilities," not only was it a mouthful, but her listener looked confused. If she said "My son is blind" or "My son is retarded," others could at least begin to understand and connect with her experience, and she was using words that accurately reflected how she herself thought about her child.

We need language to organize ourselves, but in times of social confusion and rapid change, as language itself begins to reflect those conditions, it becomes harder to know what words to use. In any event, it is dangerous to use language as a simple litmus test. Just as labels will never serve to communicate individuality, "correct" language will never be a sufficient or accurate index of what another person thinks or how she would act.

Judging

It is very easy to sit in judgment upon the behavior of others, but often difficult to realize that every judgment is a self-judgment.

—HOWARD THURMAN

A group of "special ed" parents in a suburban district became close friends over the years as their children progressed through school. When it came time for high school, one couple took exception to the practice of sending the students to another district's centralized program and, instead, persuaded their home district to permit their daughter to attend the local high school. None of the other parents joined in the request. They offered no support to the innovators and soon began to avoid them.

As parents, we are faced with decisions and choices that possess moral, ethical, and political dimensions, and whose solutions are often mutually exclusive. School and program selections fall into this category, as do choices about pregnancy, screening, termination, aggressive medical intervention, adoption, and placement away from home.

When it comes to such decisions, there is no free lunch. Not one of us makes them with ease, and whatever we decide will have painful consequences. Nevertheless, when other parents' choices are different from our own, we may feel threatened, and instead of extending empathy and support, we render judgment. Perhaps someone else's choice reawakens our doubts about our own decision, or inspires guilty feelings because we think we "should" be doing what they are doing. Conversely, we may be so convinced of the rightness of what we are doing that a different choice is incomprehensible to us.

We can release ourselves from judging ourselves and other people. Their choices are not statements about us, but only reflections of their own needs at a particular time. While we can learn from other people's experiences, our only responsibility is to make and live our own choices.

Comparisons

Every other man's war seems worse than your own.

—LOUIS SIMPSON

The mother of an extremely bright son with "low social IQ," who hits and kicks when frustrated, observes the interaction between a mother of a boy with limited intelligence and garbled speech. She thinks, "I can deal with Eric's outbursts, but I don't see how she tolerates Mark, especially when she is so brainy." Meanwhile, Mark's mother thinks to herself, "Thank God my child is not violent. I don't think I could stand that." Similarly, the father of a boy who cannot walk listens to his colleague's troubles with his chemically dependent daughter and thinks, "Now that has got to be tough."

If other families' struggles seem worse than our own, it is most likely because we are accustomed to our situation and have found ways to cope with it. When we find ourselves comparing our family with someone else's, we can use the occasion as an opportunity to step into their shoes and view our situation from the outside. No matter how unlike our own other people's lives appear to be, our differences are, in fact, only of kind and degree.

Humor

People sometimes say, "You have such strength and you've been through such tragedy." And I always remember the cartoon I drew years ago of an obese man who has fallen flat on his face and spilled all of his candy. He's thinking, "What kind of God would allow a thing like this to happen?"

—JOHN CALLAHAN, WHOSE SPINAL CORD
WAS SEVERED IN A CAR ACCIDENT

Humor, as Garrison Keillor has said, is a knife. It can be used to cut away self-pity and pain, to slice through distorted thinking, and to pierce inflated views of ourselves, letting the air out of the idea that we occupy the center of the universe. A knife is a weapon as well as a tool; it can be used to fend off attacks and senseless remarks or to make pre-emptive strikes in hostile situations.

Humor is a connector, a cushion, a buffer. It lets us get close to pain and tolerate living with it. Humor is also a vehicle for finding another perspective. Like Mary Poppins's Uncle Albert, when we start to laugh it can be "all up with us." From the vantage point of the ceiling, the room and its occupants look quite different.

Humor is an emotional Swiss Army knife: tool, weapon, vehicle, cushion, medicine, all in one, the single most versatile piece of equipment we possess.

Trust

Trust, which is a virtue, is also a habit, like prayer. It requires exercise.

—SUE HALPERN

We are keenly aware of our children's vulnerability out in the world. Whether it's because they can't see or hear, are prone to seizures, or can't accurately make change, there are many ways our children can get hurt. Our bad experiences reinforce our fear that the world—whether a neighborhood playground or a downtown street—is a hostile, unsafe place for kids like ours. To us the world has DANGER stamped all over it, and much of the time it feels too risky to permit our children to be part of it.

Yet our communities are filled with people who know, are related to, or who work with people with disabilities. We can't tell who they are just by looking at them, but they are there, passing us on the street or waiting on our table. More important, they are there when our children are out in the world on their own. While the world *is* a dangerous place, it is also a community composed of many caring and decent people. Odds are that one of them is on the bus our child rides or is standing behind her in line at the grocery store.

Today, I will put my trust in the hidden friends.

Soul Food

My nourishment comes from doing those things that I know will feed my spirit and from believing that some part of my writer's mind will be at work no matter what I am doing. So I canoe and camp and sail and garden and take walks in the woods and listen to music because I love these things and because I know that what feeds me will eventually feed my writing.

—PHYLLIS ROOT

Parenting, like writing, is a creative process that relies on the spirit. We parents cannot obtain the outcome we want by sheer will power, as if our declaring "I want to be more consistent" will make us so. Nor is parenting a matter of finding the right recipe, as if all we needed in order to obtain desired results were alter the ingredients: "Whoops! I'm a little low on patience. Guess I'll just add another cup."

In the same way that our body operates according to its rules, converting what we eat into energy, bone, and muscle, our creative process operates mysteriously and in ways only partly known to us. We cannot make the process work; we have to free it to work. Our responsibility is to feed the process: to keep the well bubbling, to keep the fire burning.

On my anxious days I will not ask what I should do, but rather what feeds me, because what feeds me feeds my work.

Dog Talk

I hate it when people talk dog talk to Mandy. You know, "Sit, Mandy."
"Good Girl." "Good job."

—DIANE, WHOSE DAUGHTER MANDY HAS RETT SYNDROME

Cathy was leaving the grocery store with her eight-year-old daughter Nancy buzzing along behind in her power chair. Heading across the parking lot, Cathy saw a car coming fast. Knowing that Nancy had a habit of zooming ahead in her chair without really looking, Cathy panicked. "Stay!" she shouted, and turned around just in time to see Nancy (who did not speak) sign W-O-O-F.

Withdrawal

The sensory problems cause the child to withdraw because the whole world hurts.

—TEMPLE GRANDIN, WHO HAS AUTISM

The child with autism withdraws because neurologically she cannot filter out sensory stimulation. Flooded with sight, sound, and feeling, she is overwhelmed, literally hurt, by sensation. She shuts down and withdraws to protect herself. Even as they recognize the cause and the logic of the withdrawal, her parents must maintain her involvement; otherwise, there is a tremendous likelihood that secondary brain damage will occur. So they engage in what Grandin, herself autistic, calls "gentle insistence." They don't push too hard, because that might result in resistance and tantrums. But they do push, in a gently insistent way, because "no pushing equals no progress."

As we become aware of the stigma and prejudice our child faces, we are overwhelmed by what we see, hear, and feel. When "the whole world hurts," we too want to withdraw, and take our child with us. But we must not withdraw, because if we do, we run the risk of causing secondary damage. Isolation, paranoia, distorted thinking, low self-esteem, and loss of confidence are the results of withdrawal. As painful as the world can be for us, we must be as gently insistent with ourselves as we are with our children. We must take them by the hand and engage the world.

No pain, no gain. No pushing, no progress.

Consciousness Raising

Are you getting your kid ready for the road, or the road ready for your kid?

—QUESTION PUT TO THE MOTHER OF A BOY WITH CYSTIC FIBROSIS WHO ADVOCATED VIGOROUSLY FOR CHANGE IN HER COMMUNITY

Getting any kid "ready for the road"—for adulthood and life on his own—is a long and arduous job that begins in infancy. Getting kids with disabilities ready is, again, even more complicated because of their needs and limitations. Not the least of the barriers our children face on the path to independent adulthood is the world's unreadiness to receive them. We begin to understand this the very first time we cannot get the wheelchair into where we are going; when the private preschool declines our toddler; when we can't find a day care mother; when the swimming instructor says she can't deal with the ear plugs.

Until recently the world thought it didn't need to make room for people with disabilities. Being separate, in an institution, living at home your whole life, not working, not being able to ride the bus or get into the store was acceptable. Society's shift to making "reasonable accommodations" and to "accessibility" is very new. And the better we parents become at adapting to our child and meeting her needs, the more we see how inept the world is, either literally or in its attitudes.

Give us the strength for another kind of readiness campaign: getting the road ready for our kids.

Stigma

It's not that easy bein' green.

—KERMIT THE FROG

It's not easy being green, even by association. As parents of children with disabilities, we are what the sociologist Erving Goffman calls "wise ones," meaning "in the know." Because of our relationship to someone who has a disability, we have a special knowledge and experience of disability, even though we are not disabled ourselves. And we react to our greenness in different ways. Some of us want to hang out almost exclusively with green folk. Some of us don't want anything to do with other green people. When we are away from our child, many of us choose to "pass," not revealing that we're really green, while others readily talk about their greenness. Whether we mostly tend to "pass" or mostly tend to "tell," there is always a choice to be made, which in itself can be wearing.

We struggle with our greenness, but our greater pain is knowing that our child has this struggle. It can be difficult for us to separate from our child, remembering that he, not we, has the disability, and that his experience of it is different from ours. As our children grow older, they will find their own ways to think about and deal with their disabilities. They may reject and criticize the ways we have characterized their disabilities and the decisions we have made for them. They may accuse us of insensitivity, failure to understand and accept, or, worse, misguided or unfair treatment. They will undoubtedly be right on some points. After all, we're not really green!

It's not easy being green. Being wise isn't easy, either.

Prejudice

I grew up on the "other side," feeling uncomfortable and afraid of people with disabilities.

—BEN ADAMS, WHOSE SON CALEB HAS HYDROCEPHALY

We experience acts of prejudice toward our child and they hurt and anger us. At the same time we may feel remorse, regret, and even guilt over the way we treated people with disabilities in the past.

We worry about how our child is treated at school because we remember how we shunned the girl in our class who didn't dress right, couldn't meet our eyes, and never gave a correct answer. We remember how we acted toward the boy down the street who used crutches, never offering to change our games so he could have a part. How "mental," "retard," and "spaz" were our favorite insults for our friends. Secure in our group, we'd run up to that unkempt guy we called Dirty Doug, say hi to him, then run away, squealing and laughing.

We remember them now and in their faces we see our son, our daughter, our friend's child. We didn't know any better then, or we didn't have the support and guidance to act differently. We can forgive ourselves for those past acts. Now we know better and we have changed.

We understand prejudice from both sides now.

Segregation

I think segregation limits kids' freedom. It limits their choices and their development. To me, "special" is another word for segregated.

—HANK, WHOSE DAUGHTER MAY HAS SIGNIFICANT DEVELOPMENTAL
DISABILITIES DUE TO UNKNOWN CAUSES

In *The Boy Who Would Be a Helicopter*, teacher Vivian Paley tells the story of Jason, a boy obsessed with toy helicopters who holds himself aloof from his classmates, remaining on the outside. "He speaks only of helicopters and broken blades, and he appears indifferent to the play and stories that surround him," Paley writes. "He has his own design for learning and, so far, it seems different from everyone else's." Jason refuses to participate in the storytelling and drama activities that are at the center of Paley's teaching methods.

Throughout the school year Paley struggles to find a way to bring Jason in. On one particularly unhappy day, when Jason is crying and running in and out of story room, torn between wanting to stay and wanting to leave, Paley takes him in her lap, wipes his tears, and asks him what he wants to do. He cannot speak for crying. As she holds him, the other children begin to make suggestions. After Jason rejects several ideas, the following occurs:

" 'Let him be in all the stories,' Joseph says.

" 'All the stories,' Alex echoes. 'Put a helicopter in every story.'

" 'Not in mine,' Lilly pouts.

" 'I mean if people want.'

"Jason stops crying and looks at the children pensively. 'Okay,' he sighs.

" 'See, he likes my idea!' Joseph is elated. 'That was in my dream, really. I was in everyone's story.' "

That is the human dream, really. To be in everyone's story, and to have everyone in our story. When we have a place in the imagination of others, we are accepted, we belong. Guided by their creative teacher, Jason's classmates found a way through dreaming, storytelling, and playacting to bring Jason, the outsider, inside. They did it by putting a helicopter in every story.

Doubt

As Adam got older, the contrast accentuated between him and other young people his age or even younger, and as this happened, I saw him retreat into solitude, take fewer risks.

—MICHAEL DORRIS, WHOSE SON ABEL HAD FETAL ALCOHOL SYNDROME. (IN HIS BOOK ABOUT ABEL, DORRIS CALLS HIM ADAM.)

The boy who played successfully on the community T-ball team and enjoyed Boy Scouts now refuses any and all offers of extracurricular activities, preferring to watch his collection of music videos and take copious notes on them. He calls it his business. He often resists joining in family outings. He used to get invited to classmates' birthday parties, but his peers no longer include him in anything outside school. If it bothers him, he doesn't let on. You throw a party, and he, who used to be the life of any party, stays in his room, listening to music.

"Well," the rationalizing voice in your head says, "he's a teenager. It's normal to want to be alone a lot. It's normal to withdraw from your family." But the doubting voice responds, "He's not doing things with peers, either. He's alone so much." The rational voice hesitates, and doubt adds, "Maybe we made a mistake taking him out of special education classes. Maybe he can't belong." Then the rationalizing voice reasserts itself: "He's an adolescent. It's a time to figure out who you are, and part of his figuring out includes dealing with his disability. Maybe the world is just too confusing right now. Maybe this withdrawal is self-protective action."

And the debate goes on, because we don't know the answer or the outcome. We don't know whether this withdrawal is the way he is going to be from now on, or whether it's part of an adolescent phase that will pass, or how things would be now if we had made different decisions in the past. We can't know for certain how much to intervene and how much to accept what we see as "the way it is." We can only pay attention, feel our way, and make the best decisions we can each day.

School Meetings

Meet tension with relaxation.

—YOGA INSTRUCTOR

People often respond in one of two ways when they meet tension or resistance to what they are trying to do: they become more aggressive or they run away. You can't get the key in the lock, so you force it, breaking the key in half. You become so frustrated by your son's constant defiance that you start yelling at him. You hate paperwork, so you avoid it and let it pile up.

Not the least of the many situations that generate tension in parents of a child with a disability is the educational planning meeting. We dread these conferences, and our fear leads to the predictable responses. Our "aggression" often takes the form of heightened emotions—we cry or shout; we run away by skipping the meeting or by attending but saying little or nothing. One parent advocate observes how seriously the anxiety of parents impairs the process in staffing meetings; it may result in plans that are much less effective than they could be. "Their anxiety makes them so uncomfortable, they just want to get out of there as fast as they can," she says.

Rarely is it helpful either to intensify and force things or run away from them. It is more useful, when encountering tension or frustration, to take a yogic approach to the situation. Yoga students learn to regard discomfort or stress as information about their bodies and to respond by staying in the pose with comfort, either by concentrating on breathing, consciously relaxing the muscles they are not using, or by being less ambitious to master the pose. If none of these works, the student may assume an easier version of the position.

The next time I feel tense about a planning meeting, I will remember that if I fight or flee, it may harm my child. I will back off from my fear or anxiety and meet it with relaxation, studying how I can stay in the process and still be comfortable.

Rights, Wants, and Needs

In the language that we share, the language of rights and duties, there is no word for giving people what they need. The words we do have, like benefits *and* entitlements, *are about granting people what they are owed, and what they are owed is limited—it is a line item in last year's budget. We are lacking the vocabulary to think in broader, more generous terms.*

—SUE HALPERN

Laws are one of the driving wedges of social change. You can't make people accept you, but backed by a law you can compel them to give you a job, or let you into school, or widen the doorways of their businesses so that you, in your wheelchair or with your low IQ, can get in. Consequently, the disability rights movement, like the feminist and black civil rights movements before it, has focused on the specific objective of securing certain rights under law for persons with disabilities.

We quickly become aware that our child has legally protected rights, and we often put a lot of energy into obtaining them. Educated by advocacy groups in the laws and how to assert them, we attempt in meetings with the school and the social service department to guarantee our child's rights by defining them in an Individual Education Plan, Individual Habilitation Plan, or Family Service Plan.

There is usually some overlap between what our child has a right to and what he wants and needs, but rights are not coextensive with needs; they are always a subset of them. And when we create rights, and speak in the language of rights, wants and needs often become secondary or even irrelevant. One of the dangers for us as parents is that we will become so caught up in rights that we forgo wants and needs. We may begin to believe that it is not enough just to need or want something, and that we can pursue what we want only when we have a legal right to it and the mechanism to secure it.

When rights become the focus of the discussions we have with those who teach and care for our child, to the exclusion of wants and needs, everyone's perception of the child, as well as the scope of the discussion, are reduced and distorted. Instead of thinking about the whole child in the context of her family and community, participants limit themselves to considering what the school has an obligation to provide or the county is minimally required to do. Who our child really is and what she wants and needs often get lost in all the paper purporting to lay out her rights.

Conflict

We have met the enemy and he is us.

—WALT KELLY, 1970 POGO CARTOON

A lot of our activities relating to our child with a disability are a struggle or feel like a struggle. There are the struggles at home: getting our son to change his shirt; keeping up with required medical care; dealing with siblings who feel resentful and left out; persisting through the extra hours it takes our daughter to complete her homework; arguing with our partner about who is doing his or her share.

There are also struggles outside the home: fielding our parents' criticism of how we handle our son; negotiating an independent living plan with the county social services; responding to the refusal of the latchkey program to accept our daughter; writing to our congresswoman about proposed changes to Medicaid; positioning ourselves in the latest power struggle going on in the advocacy organization to which we belong.

Struggle and conflict are elements of human life and endeavor. It can help enormously to recognize and accept that, and then to get some perspective on the struggle we are in. What exactly are we "fighting"? Who is the "enemy"?

Sometimes we are really struggling with ourselves: our fear, our expectations, our anxiety. We are trying to control something that is not within our power. Sometimes, especially in outside struggles, we're fighting something far bigger than ourselves. Without knowing it, we may be bucking economic, social, or political forces of which we are ignorant or only dimly aware.

As much as possible we need to know the nature of the struggle we're engaged in and who the enemy is. Insofar as "the enemy is us," we have a lot of control: we can do something about ourselves. When the "enemy" is outside us, our sphere of influence is reduced or even nonexistent. When we understand what we can control and influence and what we cannot, we know where to direct our energies, and we become much more effective at responding to conflict at every level.

Relentless

It is not true that life is one damn thing after another—it's one damn thing over and over.

—EDNA ST. VINCENT MILLAY

Shave him. Have the daily conversation in which you persuade him to put on clean clothes. Floss his teeth. Change the diaper. Do the bowel program. Send him back for another shower. "And this time wash your hair!" Take him to the doctor for treatment of the mosquito bite that has become infected from being scratched. One mother says, "Sometimes I feel that my whole job as a parent just comes down to hygiene."

When children are small, we expect to be intimately involved with their bodily functions and personal care. But as our child with a disability grows older, we become more conscious of how out of the ordinary it is to have to take care of someone else's physical needs every day. It is demanding, relentless, and repetitive, the kind of work that is never finished. What did Yogi Berra say? "It's déjà vu all over again."

Confidence

Of all the qualities in a manager conducive to innovation and initiative, a degree of uncertainty may be the most powerful. If a manager is confident but uncertain—confident that the job will get done but without being certain of exactly the best way of doing it—employees are likely to have more room to be creative, alert, and self-starting.

—ELLEN J. LANGER

It seems that we often mix up certainty and confidence; we tend to think that certainty is confidence. Or it may be that the lower our confidence, the greater our tendency to seek refuge in certainty. We want to know the precise diagnosis, the best therapy regimen, what kind of program a child should have if she has qualities A, B, and C; what she will be like when she's three, ten, twenty.

Often we are encouraged in this quest for certainty by the people around us. We are in the process of making a difficult decision about using aggressive medical treatment, and our mother says, "I think the only thing to do is . . ." The school personnel defend a classroom choice we have reservations about by asserting, "Research shows that a child like Marissa must have . . ."

Certainty and dogmatic attitudes act like screens, blocking out information and interfering with our awareness of other ways of doing things. If we, or those with whom we are dealing, are committed to the truth or necessity of one viewpoint, we feel no impetus to consider another one. Indeed, we are more likely to defend and justify what has become our position.

In lieu of so much certainty, what we really need, in ourselves and others, is open-mindedness, the freedom to make and acknowledge mistakes, and a sense that there is room for risks. As Ellen

Langer's business research shows, innovation is far more likely to take place where these qualities of uncertainty exist.

Our uncertainty need not undermine our sense of confidence, which is based on our past experiences. These confirm that life goes on, the job gets done, we have the ability to handle new problems and situations, and we are, in fact, raising our child.

When we see that confidence based on certainty is false confidence, we will feel more comfortable with uncertainty, and will become more creative and effective at solving whatever crops up.

Recurring Sorrow

Sorrow was like the wind. It came in gusts.

—MARJORIE KINNAN RAWLINGS

Bob comes home from work on the last day of school to find that all his kids have gone to parties and overnights with friends, except Daniel, his son with a disability, who is distraught because his clumsy efforts to arrange something have failed. "I really need an overnight here, Dad," says Daniel. The fabric of an otherwise ordinary day tears open, and Daniel's words drop like molten lead on his father's heart. Bob takes Daniel out to supper that night and feels sad all evening because his sixteen-year-old's social life depends so heavily on him. But the next day he gets out the schedule for summer activities at the community center and helps Daniel find a class he's interested in. He and Daniel set up a date for Daniel's friend John to stay overnight, and Bob stands by while Daniel calls John, then gets on the phone to confirm the plan with John's mother.

The emotions do not fade. The intense sorrow and grief we felt when we first found out about our child's disability lives on in us and, like the emotions connected with other significant events in our life, will continue to be exposed by unexpected words or events. We cannot choose the moments when the covering of everyday life will tear and we will feel that first pain afresh. The rips will catch us unexpectedly, arising out of the most mundane events. There is really no way to anticipate or avoid them.

And we needn't wish to avoid these moments of hurt, because

they tell us we are alive—alive to our own life experience, and alive to our child and to everything about him. The part of us tender enough to feel that pain is the same part that enables us to respond to our child's feelings, love him, and take action on his behalf.

Cat Trick

Make not your sail too big for your ballast.

—ENGLISH PROVERB

Remember the Cat in the Hat, glibly standing on a ball while he triumphantly balanced an ever-growing tower of objects?

"Look at me! Look at me! Look at me NOW!" he exulted just before he crashed to the floor, bringing the whole mess down with him.

What brought the Cat in the Hat down? Lack of skill? Adding new things without dropping others? Maybe it was the impossible hat itself, or being too busy showing off. Perhaps it was because he wouldn't listen to Sally and her brother, or that fount of common sense, the fish. Then again, it may have been because he was standing on a ball instead of planting his feet on firm ground.

If the hat fits, wear it.

Depression

I feel like a fraud saying I'm fine. I'm fine and not fine, all at once.

—MOTHER BEING TREATED FOR DEPRESSION

Once there was a woman who had two young children, one extremely bright, always bubbling over with complex questions like a fountain. The other child had Down syndrome. A lawyer by training, this mother worked part time in an effort to keep her skills current and because she enjoyed what she did. Her husband was away a great deal on business trips, and she was the primary caretaker of her children as well as an active advocate for her disabled son. One week this woman's mother came for a visit. After watching her daughter in action for a few days, the mother sincerely observed, "I don't know how you do it all." "I work fourteen hours a day!" the daughter snapped back.

Indeed, she hit the floor running when she got up at 7 A.M. and scarcely paused before 9 at night. She was tired all the time. She hardly ever did anything that was fun. But she kept going. In fact, she kept it all going for an amazingly long time.

And then one winter she, who rarely even caught a cold, started to get sick a lot. One infection followed another. She found herself crying for no reason. Driving home or in a department store, she would suddenly feel tears well up. More days than not when her husband came home from work he found the kids in front of the TV in a darkening house and his wife asleep on the couch. She cut back on her work hours and saw a therapist every week, but it didn't help. Every time she turned around she seemed to be excusing herself from a board meeting or begging for an extension on a project. Her life became a round of apologies and failures.

Finally she found her way to a psychiatrist who diagnosed her with depression and began treating her with antidepressant medication. Spring came, the medication helped, and she began to feel better and to gain some perspective on herself and her life.

She realized slowly that her recovery was not just a matter of taking a pill, as vital as that pill was for a time. Recovery meant taking a walk every day, going to a support group meeting, taking more time for herself, resting, playing. She decided she would take a vacation from disability advocacy. She would not write one letter. She resigned from all her boards, took a sabbatical from her job, and told her husband he was going to have to attend the special education meetings with her and share in addressing their son's school issues.

She started taking piano lessons. She took a lot of naps and read good books. She began to go to church again. It had taken years for her to get as sick as she was, and it took more than a year for her to get well. But she did.

When I take on too much, neglect myself, or consistently subordinate my needs to those of others, I leave myself vulnerable to depression. Today, I will make it a priority to meet my own needs so that I can stay mentally and emotionally healthy and be the person, partner, and parent I want to be.

Prenatal Screening

Your physician, a clergyperson, geneticists, co-workers, counselors and friends cannot tell you what to do, even though you may be tempted to seek an answer from them or they may offer answers.

—SHEROKEE ILSE

You are pregnant again, and because you already have a child with a disability you are going to have to make decisions about prenatal screening and possibly about termination. Maybe you are already absolutely clear about what you are willing to do and not do. More likely you are filled with fears, doubt, and ambivalence. Whatever certainties you possess may begin to crumble as you go through the process.

Ultimately, your decisions are intensely personal and private, yet from the beginning you will be making them "in public." There will be consultations with professionals who are strangers to you; there will be advice and opinions from family members, co-workers, and even casual acquaintances. There will be those who question why you ventured another pregnancy.

Along the way, whatever you do, some of the people you love may be pained, disappointed, and even angered by your decisions. Some may withdraw their support because they do not agree with you. It is a time to be with those who love you no matter what.

To get pregnant or not; to refuse testing or screening; to accept screening and any risk it entails even if you are unsure about what you would do with what you learn; to terminate or continue your pregnancy—you have a right to make all of these decisions, and they are yours and yours alone to make. Trust that when you get to each of them your instincts will guide you to what is right for you.

Remember that you do not owe anyone justifications or explanations.

You will endure an experience you would prefer to avoid. You will be faced with choices you wish you did not have to make. Only you will live these moments and their consequences. Be square with yourself. Nothing and no one else matters.

Chronic Sickness

The end of March came. April began. Still the storm was there, waiting a little longer now perhaps, but striking even more furiously. There was the bitter cold still, and the dark storm days, the wheat to be ground, the hay to be twisted. Laura seemed to have forgotten summer; she could not believe it would ever come again.

—LAURA INGALLS WILDER

Whether a serious illness causes our child to be disabled, or the disability our child has is accompanied by certain illnesses, chronic sickness is often part of our life with our child. Even though the sickness is not extreme or dangerous in itself, when it is chronic it places extraordinary demands on the family and each of its members. The child cannot go to school and falls behind; the parents miss work; social engagements are canceled; the other children lack attention; the house is not maintained. Worry intensifies as we see the secondary physical effects of persistent illness and of medication. Financial pressures mount because of direct medical costs and lost wages.

"I felt that we lived in a box," says one mother. "When Gloria was not sick, the lid was open, and we could go in and out of the box, but when she got sick, the lid slammed shut. We were isolated in this dark, limited space defined by the illness. At first, I fought it and put my energy into trying to get the box open. But soon I gave in to it—what else can you do?—and started to figure out how to turn on some lights and cut a window in the box."

Limbo

The feeling of being in "limbo" is itself a loss. Even if the situation turns out fine . . . while in doubt that doubt is a loss and should be treated accordingly.

—MELBA COLGROVE, HAROLD BLOOMFIELD, AND PETER MCWILLIAMS

In Roman Catholic theology limbo is the place reserved for souls that, though not condemned to hell, are barred from heaven because they have not been baptized. Today when we talk about limbo, we mean being in a situation where things are uncertain and undecided and could go either of two dramatic ways. The outcome could be heaven—or hell.

We are in limbo when we are waiting for amniocentesis results or the report on our child's assessment. We are in limbo while our newborn struggles each moment for life in the incubator, when our son is having his open heart surgery, when our daughter is on the waiting list for a community placement. If we're in a lawsuit with our school district, trying to sell our house so that we can move to a community with the services our child needs, or considering divorce, we are in limbo.

When we are in limbo we live every day with doubt; we don't know where to pitch our emotions. The coin is in the air. How do we call the toss? Anything we say or feel is a guess.

If my life is in limbo I must recognize and accept the way I feel as normal and necessary. I will do my best to accept that today I must live with uncertainty.

Heroism

And as the parent of an autistic child, one is more ridiculous than heroic—like a sludging, sloshing infantry soldier in a nuclear age.

—JOSH GREENFELD

To me, the most interesting aspect of any heroic feat is what change it allows spiritually.

—CHRISTINA BALDWIN

We don't feel heroic. Our kids are called special, but we don't really think we are. And we don't want to be. We just want to be ordinary people, like everyone else. Normal.

In fact, as Josh Greenfeld says, more than anything else, we are likely to feel ridiculous as we plod along changing diapers on a ten-year-old, picking up after another tantrum, literally spending years helping someone learn to make change for a dollar. Everyone else is on a jet plane, and we're walking. Foolish—that's how we feel.

Ironically, walking is the heroic feat. Getting up every day, day after day, and walking while the planes soar overhead. In spite of feelings of foolishness, fatigue, even futility, our keeping on, one foot after the other, is what constitutes our heroism.

And then comes the really interesting question: What change does this allow for me spiritually?

Funky

[Brice] had died during delivery and was resuscitated seven minutes later, and so was born a second time, but it turned out that he had been gone too long. His eyes were deep gray, and always open, and he never cried or, for that matter, smiled, or even blinked . . .

"He's a good baby," Sam told me one day in the car, after we'd been reading to Brice for a while. "But he's a little funky."

—ANNE LAMOTT

It would take a precocious California four-year-old to come up with the right word. If only it could catch on. We could subscribe to *Funky Parent* magazine. Our kids could get services from Funky Education and the Funky Services Division of the Department of Funkiness. They could be taught by funky teachers. They could use funky equipment. We could attend conferences of the National Association of Funky Kids and the Association for Persons with Severe Funkiness.

All our kids are good kids. But they are a little funky. In sad, hilarious, frustrating, gratifying, amusing, heartbreaking, boring, touching, and always unique ways—they're funky, all right.

PART THREE

Transformed

There is always hope says
Mehitabel
if you don't weaken.

—DON MARQUIS, "HOLD EVERYTHING,"
the lives and times of archy and mehitabel

Inevitably, over time, things change. Some problems we solve; some issues go away. We move into a better school district; our child grows up and becomes more self-sufficient; a health problem is resolved. Other aspects of our parenting, though they may present themselves in different guises, will never go away. There will always be certain unanswerable questions and doubts. Conflict, mistakes, and failure will remain because they are consistent components of any worthwhile endeavor. Our lives will be complicated, always tempting us to overload and overdo. Because of our children's extra and extraordinary needs— we may be their eyes, ears, voice, legs—it may be hard for us to let go and get out of their way or to free ourselves of responsibilities we are ready to put down.

Surely by now we know that we have the power to influence and change the political and social reality. Each of us is repeatedly presented with the opportunity for useful political and social action and must decide, again and again, whether, when, and how we will accept that challenge. In politics and all the other realms of our child's life our issue becomes one of endurance and stamina. Can we last?

Sooner or later we learn that determination, will power, household help, therapy, activism, parent groups, escapes, and all other outside support we may rely on aren't enough. Real staying power comes from trading activity for stillness, and turning to the oasis within ourselves, the "surface of no strain," which is the only true source of renewal.

We come to a new place where we discover that we have been opened to love and transformed. We have new ways of seeing our creator, our child, our own humanity, and the rest of mankind. We have lived and learned the great human paradox—that out of pain, sorrow, disappointment, and failure are forged growth, power, strength, and love.

Fading

It's amazing to me that this boy, with such a profound handicap of the brain, can continue to deepen his music. For a long time, I felt that it was my role to express things for him, but now he can do it on his own. It turns out that I overestimated my role.

—KENZABURO OE, WHOSE SON HIKARI IS BRAIN DAMAGED

Kenzaburo Oe's prize-winning fiction is based on his life with his son, Hikari, whose compositions for flute and piano have been recorded and are highly admired. Hikari, who was brain damaged at birth, has seizures, rarely speaks, and needs constant care. Yet Hikari can express himself through music, and his father, in spite of having won a Nobel Prize for his fiction, decided to stop writing. He realized that he didn't need to speak for Hikari anymore.

Few of us have children who possess both profound handicaps and soaring talent, and most of us do not possess anything approaching Nobel-level abilities, yet there is much for us in the Oes' story. For who among us has not overestimated his role in his child's life, and perhaps in so doing blocked or inhibited her from fully developing her capacities? How many of us haven't known when to give up or to alter the part we play?

Our motives are good and often spring from our desire to protect. We don't want our children to totally flop when they give a speech to the class, so we write it for them, ignoring that we are cheating them of their ideas or the way they would express them. Someone speaks to them, and because we are afraid they won't be understood, we answer for them. Their choice of clothes is unusual, so we dictate what they wear. We go to meetings and presume to say what our children are thinking and feeling. It is scary for us to let them approach the world on their own terms.

On the long road that parent and child travel from total dependence to independence, every parent is at times going to keep playing a role that is no longer needed. Each of us will overestimate his own part or be a little slow to catch on that it's time to step back. With our child who depends on us more than usual, for longer than usual, we are much more likely to make and persist in these mistakes.

Let me not get between my child and what he is seeking to tell the world.

Prediction

The message we want to get out is that you judge Down's people just like anyone else; that child, when he is born, is as unknown as any child.

—PATRICIA HEATH, WHOSE SON PHILIP HAS DOWN SYNDROME

With our normal kids, we approach the future as unknown and fill it in with our own happy fantasies. We cherish the illusion that they will always be all right, that everything will turn out for the best. We see their talents and abilities and dream of doctors and dancers, astronauts and presidents. Although we have moments of fear and worry, we do not count on there being bad things in store for them. In the bright landscape of our minds there are no serious accidents, terminal illnesses, or violent crimes. We do not persistently imagine their teen and adult years plagued by bad grades, chemical dependency, depression, or failed relationships. However, when it comes to our child with a disability, we press to know the whole child now, including what her future will be. Instead of nurturing dreams inspired by her talents and abilities, we entertain nightmares fueled by her lacks and limitations.

To imagine one child's future without pain or problems is as mistaken as believing that another child has no gifts or potential. Between these two extremes lies a more valuable awareness: we do not possess or own any of our children. They are not us. Their futures are not ours to predict and control. Our job is to discover who they are in the time they are with us and prepare them as best we can for the lives that are theirs to live.

Our challenge is to meet each child, when she is born, as un-known, a stranger who is our guest, to draw out her gifts and lead her into her future, with its light and dark, its pain and promise, its limitations and its possibilities.

Empowerment

*Still, the most enduring legacy of militant moms is their militant kids.
Having watched how their parents fought for them, many disabled people
grow up to be forceful self-advocates.*

—JOSEPH P. SHAPIRO

At a parent-training conference Carla found herself seated at the
dinner table next to the disability rights activist Ed Roberts, the
founder of the Independent Living Centers. As they talked about
Carla's son, Troy, who was six and could not walk, Ed asked
whether Troy had a power wheelchair. "Well, no," answered Carla,
who had never even thought of such a thing. "What?" said Ed.
"Are you one of those controlling moms or something?" "I *was* a
controlling mom," Carla said later. "I thought I was supposed to be.
I thought that was my job, keeping everything under control and
safe. It took me a long time and a big push from Ed to realize safe is
not what it's about."

Troy got his power chair. One day he took a tumble in the street.
His glasses flew off, and a passing car drove over them. At the
sound of his loud crying, Carla rushed outside, sure that he was
upset and scared, praying that he was not hurt. But Troy was not
scared; he was angry. The tears were tears of outrage. "Mom, that
guy ran over my glasses and he didn't even stop! Let's call Ed
Roberts. He'll get him!"

When Carla got Troy a motorized wheelchair, she powered
much more than his movements. She powered his sense of himself.
And that is our most important job: powering our child's sense of
himself.

Discovery

In many ways, Aaron has been transforming me over the years by simply being unable to do things my way. I have to either give up on him or open to the different ways he can do things, and the different things he can do.

—VICKIE NOBLE, WHOSE SON AARON HAS DOWN SYNDROME

Living with difference, like immersion in another culture, causes us to re-evaluate our concepts of normality and to question our assumptions about who we are and why we are the way we are. In the altered landscape of our home we find that we can no longer depend on language, facial expressions, behaviors, or thought patterns that up to now we always took for granted. We are compelled to find another way to recognize the hunger of a baby who does not cry, and forced to discover new ways to play with a child who cannot see.

A teenage girl says it fascinates her when she gets a glimpse of how her autistic sister's mind works. "It gets me wondering about how I think or how anyone thinks. The brain is really amazing." When, like anthropologists, we approach our child with a spirit of openness and curiosity, we learn how to understand him and live with him. We also acquire, and can bring to the world, new insight and an enlarged understanding of what it means to be a human being.

Celebration

Become trigger-happy about celebrations. On days when your child "makes it" and does something better than he or she ever did it before, call others in . . . and throw a party!

—ROBERT PERSKE

A couple who voluntarily acted as legal guardians for a man with developmental disabilities found themselves embroiled in a lengthy and bitter legal battle with their county over what services should be provided for him. At one point the county petitioned to remove the couple as guardians. When the judge decided the couple should remain, and made other decisions helpful to the man's cause, the guardians gave a thank-you dinner for the many people who had been involved and had helped them over the years of litigation. The couple found that to sit down and compile the list, to send invitations that said "thank you, please come," was in itself a tremendous affirmation. In a situation that had created intense hostility, and had wounded and exhausted them, they found solace in focusing on their friends and on their gains, and in joining the two for celebration.

Is there an occasion for celebration? Did my daughter dress herself today? Did my son pass his five-year cancer check-up? Did we finally get a van with a lift? Let me invite someone to share it.

Safety

Freedom is not free.

SLOGAN FROM A 1960s ARMY RECRUITING POSTER

Our realistic acceptance of our child's disability teaches us that her freedom to do what she wants in life is compromised. Our awareness of her vulnerability teaches us to be extravigilant and cautious. Our fears about what could happen to her entice us to limit our dreams and opt for safety.

As Louis the trumpeter swan says to the zookeeper who is extolling the advantages of the zoo, "Safety is all well and good: I prefer freedom." To help our child enjoy all the freedom she can, we must take up arms against fear. We have to take risks and encourage our child to take them. If she doesn't learn to take calculated risks while still under our care and guidance, how will she be able to do so when we are not there, or not there all the time? Without practice, how will she know which risks are reasonable and worth taking, and which are foolish or too dangerous?

Whether it's going to the junior high dance, getting a power wheelchair, giving a speech to the class about what it's like to have cerebral palsy, going away to camp, applying for a job, taking a class outside the special education classroom, getting an apartment, taking a trip alone—whatever it is, I will not let my fear stand in the way of my child's freedom.

Surprise

Trust in the unexpected—

—EMILY DICKINSON

A young man who was mentally handicapped loved TV mystery shows and had a habit of recounting each plot to his family, even when they had watched the show with him. One night they saw a dramatization of an Agatha Christie story involving a man who had invited a guest to dinner and wound up dead in his own study. Afterward, Benjamin launched into his description of the plot and the characters, recounting the clues with great detail and drama. His family ground their teeth and bit their tongues as he talked about the victim's cat (part of a humorous subplot), the sequence of events, and each dish that had been served at the dinner—the chicken, the salad, the dessert soufflé. Benjamin finally approached the conclusion, poised to share his solution to the mystery. "And then"—he paused for dramatic effect—"guess what?" His family waited for him to say that the victim had been murdered by the man who came to dinner. But after another pause, he announced with a flourish, "The cat ate the soufflé!"

The Missing Piece

Once, ready to try anything, I made an appointment to see an Indian guru over on the other side of town . . . He said, "Listen, my son. You are fortunate."

"What do you mean?"

"You are in an excellent position for spiritual growth."

Fuck spiritual growth, I thought. I wanted to feel my own body, jump around, and be free of these crazy attendants.

—JOHN CALLAHAN, WHOSE SPINAL CORD WAS
SEVERED IN A CAR ACCIDENT

A woman whose child had a disability had a good friend, Vivian, who lived a deeply spiritual life. Watching her friend's struggles and distress, Vivian gently attempted to introduce her to the idea that something was missing from her life. She invited her to come along to her church, which was the same denomination her friend had been raised in. The friend criticized the shallowness of the sermon all the way home. Vivian gave her friend a short, powerful book on the spiritual life, but her friend never got around to reading it. Undeterred, Vivian asked her friend, "What about your spiritual life?" Her friend said, "I'm really not into religion anymore." Fuck spirituality.

Years later, after a time of great crisis, the friend began to get a glimmer, through a twelve-step program, of the meaning and necessity of a spiritual dimension in her life. She began to understand that she couldn't solve everything intellectually or by sheer force of her ego. She saw that it was necessary to acknowledge something larger than herself, and that only when her life was centered in an

212

awareness and reverence for that larger something would she be free from her grief, anger, and resentment.

She and Vivian no longer live in the same state and have not corresponded in years, but recently when she found the book Vivian gave her and read it with appreciation, she sent out a mental message: "Thank you, Viv. Your gift has been received."

Yielding

It helps to resign as the controller of your fate. All that energy we expend
to keep things running right is not what's keeping things running right.

—ANNE LAMOTT

Looking at what might be ours if we surrender to the fact of our child's disability and its impact on our life, looking around at the roles others in a similar position seem to occupy, we might immediately protest: Hey, wait a minute. I don't want to be exceptional, special, an advocate, political, a pioneer, a teacher, an expert on disability, brave, anguished, stigmatized, toughened, changed, holy.

To surrender means to yield to the power of another; it carries strong connotations of defeat and ignominy. But to surrender also means to give up resistance. When we cling to our self-will we are in the ludicrous position of putting ourselves in charge of things that are out of our control. On the other hand, when we give up our will, when we give up resisting something we can't change anyway, we open ourselves to a new set of choices. Actually, we never abandon our ability to will and to choose. We only shed the will we are presently exerting, because it no longer fits the circumstances of our life. Like a molting lobster, we give up the too-small will and grow a new set of intentions that fit.

Having given up our will that our child will walk, or see, or go to college, or continue the family name, having embraced the new choices and undertaken new actions, we may discover that what we are doing is, in fact, exceptional or pioneering. We may find that our new, bigger shell *is* that of an advocate or an expert.

Oasis

For one who has chosen the desert and truly embraced the forsaken ground it is not despair or fear or limitation that dictates how one lives. One finds instead an openness and hope that verges on the wild.

—KATHLEEN NORRIS

Parenting a child with a disability is like living in the desert; it is the same as any parenting, but in a more exacting environment. Most of us did not choose to live here, but if we can accept it as if we had chosen it, if we can "truly embrace the forsaken ground," we will find that we can live this life, not in despair and fear, but with openness and hope. We will find, as Kathleen Norris did on the high Plains, that we can "be in the desert and let it bloom."

To do this we need a source of renewal, an oasis, a place where our spirit finds water, food, shade, and rest. Living in the desert becomes the occasion, the impetus, the opportunity for us to discover our oasis. So that one day, assessing our experience as the parent of a child with a disability, we may say, with Kathleen Norris: "As it turns out, the Plains have been essential not only for my growth as a writer; they have formed me spiritually. I would even say they have made me a human being."

Today, I will realize that where I am offers me a way to my full humanness, to my full being.

Serenity

God wants nothing of you but the gift of a peaceful heart.

—MEISTER JOHANNES ECKHART

My goal is a peaceful heart, a calm mind. My goal is to remain serene though the earth rocks around me. My serenity is mine to neglect or develop. This is one area where my efforts to change will have results. I am the ruler of my inner state of being.

I can choose how to respond to outside events. I can decide to get wildly upset over a newspaper article or a TV show that depicts people with disabilities in a mistaken or insensitive light, or I can choose to stay calm, consider what I could do, and decide whether or not to take action. I can even elect not to watch the show. I can permit my child's every up and down to determine my emotional state for the day, or I can make a commitment to being even-keeled, riding the waves of my own sea, not someone else's.

Today, I make a commitment to my serenity. I will examine ways to increase my sense of calm and self-possession. I may choose to attend church, run, work in my garden, set aside time to pray or meditate, practice my music, take a walk, make something, or participate in a support group or recovery circle.

I will recognize my serenity for the precious treasure that it is. I will protect and care for it more than anything I possess.

Harmony

I finally figured out that time is something to keep, not keep up with.

—AN ADULT PIANO STUDENT

Music is governed by rhythm, time, and tempo. Musicians accept as axiomatic that they always have to make the music fit the rhythm. The beat is all. In our hurry-up culture most of us base our days on the clock, and regard time as something we have to keep up with— or even ahead of. If we could only listen for the natural rhythm that is embedded in our lives, we would find it easier to be clear about our priorities, including the need to rest and relax. Instead of *keeping up* with our day, feeling rushed and stressed, we could then move and act *in time* with our day, feeling calm and focused. While many days call for the steady discipline of march time or the rapid pace required by *presto*, others are *andante*, walking tempo, or are in the lilting one, two, three of waltz time. If we find and honor the rhythm of our days, our lives will become more harmonious.

Orientation

How we spend our days is, of course, how we spend our lives. What we do with this hour, and that one, is what we are doing.

—ANNIE DILLARD

Rise up in the morning, face the East, then sit quietly and get your bearings before launching into this unknown day. What action does the day call for? What choices do you have about what you will and will not do? What is most important? Consult your inner weather. What are you thinking and feeling? What is worrying or agitating you? Can you give it up? What, today, are you thankful for? Will you celebrate it? Before you set out, make these two simple lists, enumerating what you will give up and what you are thankful for.

Today, I give up: my fear, my anxiety, my frustration, my irritability, my habit of focusing on what is wrong, my sense of not having enough.

Today, I am thankful for: the sunshine, my job, my home, the people I live with, the people I love, those who love me.

Cross-Over

There is a place at the center of earth
where one ocean dissolves inside the other
in a black and holy love;
It's why the whales of one sea
know songs of the other,
why one thing becomes something else
and sand falls down the hourglass
into another time.

—LINDA HOGAN

In the sand counties of central Wisconsin, two areas with different flora—different plant life—meet and overlap. To the south stretches Illinois and a province of prairies, oak savannas, and southern hardwoods; northward to Canada extend pine savannas, conifer-hardwoods, and boreal forest. Botanists describe such a boundary as a "tension zone," which is typically very diverse and resilient in its plant and animal life.

Our family constitutes a zone of cultural overlap, a tension zone where the stigmatized, the "other," who were traditionally cast out, live with the nonstigmatized and through them participate in the dominant culture. Our homes are on the cultural edge, the cross-over zone, whose inhabitants live at the outer limits of what is socially sanctioned. What is true about botanical tension zones also holds true for us: "While for particular individuals existence at the limits of their range entails great risk, for the community as a whole the remarkable diversity of such a zone provides greater resiliency and opportunity for adjustment to change."

Our home is the place where the ocean of the stigmatized dissolves into the ocean of the not-stigmatized, where "they" become "we," where the past becomes the future, and whales sing across the seas to one another.

Privacy

I might have been a goldfish in a glass bowl for all the privacy I got.

—SAKI (H. H. MUNRO)

Seven night nurses and four personal care attendants rotate in shifts, night and day, at the Smith household, providing the medical monitoring and daily care and assistance that their son, Lee, needs. Ann and Will Smith have lived this way for five years, ever since they agreed to the aggressive medical measures that saved Lee, born fourteen weeks premature.

For those of us whose child's intensive needs require many helpers, the choice to keep our child at home often means giving up a private life. Instead, we live a life where other people are always hearing our fights, where we never feel the relaxation of being completely alone, where we can't go into the kitchen at night in our underwear. For some of us this life was unthinkable or intolerable, and sealed our decision to have our child cared for somewhere else. Others of us have decided to try to live in the goldfish bowl.

Within our 360 degrees of visibility, we learn to construct our miniature castles of privacy built of nights out together and clear personal boundaries. We survive in the goldfish bowl and keep our family intact.

The Whole Story

Pictures lie. They don't tell the whole picture.

—EDDIE ADAMS

The family pictures we take are true in themselves, but they tell only pieces of the story. Here are Mom and Dad gazing raptly at their newborn daughter. Here is Katy on her first birthday, with frosting all over her face. Here she holds her new baby sister, and following that there are pages of the girls sledding, building block towers, playing in the sand. Holiday scenes filled with dress-up clothes, presents, relatives, and festive meals accumulate. We see Katy getting on the school bus and having a swimming lesson. Here, she and two classmates grin proudly as they hold up their track and field ribbons.

But there are no photographs of the 150 missed days of school; of Dad lying awake at night, worrying about Katy's future; of Mom going all over town trying to find shoes that fit; or of the long, difficult struggle with the school district. There are no pictures of Katy lost at the mall, or never being invited for an overnight at a friend's house, or spending hours on homework. None of these became a Kodak moment. For the whole story we need all the pictures, the ones we save in our albums and those imprinted in our minds and hearts alone.

Language

"When I use a word," Humpty Dumpty said in rather a scornful tone,"
it means just what I choose it to mean—neither more nor less."

"The questions is," said Alice, "whether you can make words mean
so many different things."

"The questions is," said Humpty Dumpty, "which is to be master—
that's all."

—LEWIS CARROLL

Not the least of our problems as the parents of a child with a
disability is what language to use when we think and talk about
him and our experience. Changes in the attitudes toward, and
treatment of, people with disabilities have been reflected in
changes in the language used to describe them. In the nineteenth
century the clinical terms for a person with developmental disabilities included "idiot," "imbecile," and "moron." At the beginning of
this century "feeble-minded" was the preferred term, giving way
after World War II to "mentally retarded," which is now being
abandoned in favor of "cognitively impaired" or "developmentally
disabled."

Arc, the national organization for persons with developmental
disabilities, founded in the late 1940s, first called itself the Association for Retarded Children, reflecting both its identity as a
parent group and the common practice of referring to individuals
with developmental disabilities as "children," no matter what
their age.

In the 1960s this attitude came to be seen as inaccurate and
demeaning, leading the organization to change its name to the
Association for Retarded Citizens, and then to change again in the

1980s—to the Arc—after adult members who were developmentally disabled protested the term "retarded." Those same members are now euphemistically called "self-advocates" to distinguish them from members with "normal" intellectual functioning, thus sadly testifying to a continuing need to separate through language.

We may not care about theories of language or how language affects social policy. Yet we find ourselves in a situation where the words we need to talk about our child are hotly debated, constantly changing, and charged with political meaning. What words do we use? Mentally retarded or developmentally disabled? Disabled or differently abled? Blind or visually impaired? For those of us with children who have any sort of disability, the question of labels hits closest to home when we want to describe our child to someone. We may decide to refer to our son as a "chromosomally differentiated youth," but it's doubtful that will catch on.

But perhaps, as John Hockenberry argues in *Moving Violations*, the search for simple names is itself a mistake. "The obsession with finding the right name," he writes, "leads us away from the unique. The whole is diminished by ignoring its parts." The shorthand of labels will never convey the unique capacities, incapacities, and nature of our child, and the convenience of categories will always distort and flatten the detailed specifics that constitute actual experience. Nor will changing the label eradicate the underlying stigma, though it may alert speakers to the stigma and its reinforcement or enhancement by language.

Labels invite people to experience the individual with a disability solely in terms of his need and dysfunction, leading to a predominant perception of helplessness. They provide a mere outline of the person, on which the listener can project his beliefs, ideas, fears, and fantasies. Categories and pigeonholes create distance, allowing others to avoid knowing and engaging the individual with a disability on his own terms.

When I call my child by name and talk about him in terms of who he is, what he can do and give, and what he needs, I evoke, both for myself and for others, a real, three-dimensional person living a real life.

Adversity

It is a curious circumstance that only pines in full sunlight are bitten by weevils; shaded pines are ignored. Such are the hidden uses of adversity.

—ALDO LEOPOLD

For a pine tree a shady location is undesirable, because pines grow best in full sunlight. But somehow shaded pines are immune from attack by weevils, which eat their candles and prevent them from growing properly. When it comes to weevils, shaded trees have an advantage.

In many ways our child's disability is an undesirable circumstance in her life and in the life of our family. But what are the "hidden uses" of this adversity? What opportunities does an adverse situation offer our family, if we can only open our eyes to the possibilities?

I have learned things about how a child grows and develops that have made me a better parent to all my children. I have been led to a new career. I have met many wonderful people and made new friends. I grew up. My children are tolerant and compassionate. I am closer to God.

As Aldo Leopold learned from his careful observations of nature, everything is connected, everything serves a purpose in the larger scheme of things.

Today, I will think about the hidden uses of life in the shade.

Endless Goals

If you do not make your goal the first time, do not give up or quit. Size up the task and try it again in a new way. Try to focus on what will help you make your rate the next time. It may be that you need just to slow down in order to speed up.

—JERRY W. ROBINSON, APPLIED KEYBOARDING

In our lives with our children there will be a procession of goals, some of them quite difficult: securing an appropriate school program; stabilizing their health; teaching them to dress themselves. Some of these goals, though related to our children and their special needs, will be personal: making some time for ourselves in every day; learning to be more effective at meetings; getting more help in the house.

We probably won't reach all of our goals the first time we try, or achieve each of them with equal ease. Here's where a little typing wisdom comes in handy: "Do not give up or quit. Size up the task and try it again in a new way." Remember, the typist who can barrel along at sixty words a minute has no success if the copy is full of mistakes. Typing success requires speed *and* accuracy. The typing student who learns to slow down a little to gain accuracy comes up with a better rate than the error-ridden speed demon.

When we feel we are not achieving our goals and are tempted to push harder and go faster, it may be that we need to ease up in order to make progress.

Intensification

Why make big problems out of little problems?

—P. D. EASTMAN

From the kitchen window a mother watches her nine-year-old son and his friend playing in the driveway. They have newspaper and a magnifying glass and very soon they have a fire. As she heads out to intervene, the mother thinks how like a magnifying glass the effect of her other son's disability is on their family. It often causes ordinary, everyday things—her love for her child, a temper tantrum, a worry, what someone else said—to become intensified, transformed, powerful, and even dangerous.

We need to pay attention to this intensifying phenomenon in our lives. The next time we find our days and nights disturbed by worries of how our child will adjust to school or how our anger was triggered by a caseworker's comment, we can take away the magnifier and reduce the problem to normal dimensions. The next time a neighbor exaggerates our child's "misbehavior," or our mother in her anxiety keeps telling us what to do, we can pause and put it in perspective. The next time our child's difficult behavior has the family in an uproar, we can step back and think how to defuse the situation so that sunshine and a newspaper don't become a conflagration.

Fire is a valuable and crucial resource if we don't burn ourselves when using it. We can consciously call on the intensifying effect of our child's disability when we need it to emphasize a truth or put fire into our words, and we can learn to consciously put down the magnifying glass when it serves no good end.

Blessing

One man's paralyzing trauma is another man's invitation to take control of his life; one woman's grounds for insanity is another woman's goad to a dramatic shaping of the self.

—ROSELLEN BROWN

Is having a child with a disability a curse or a blessing? A cross or an anchor? A barrier to what I really want to do, or a lightning rod for my priorities? At different times it is probably each of these things, but our attitude can tip the balance, one way or the other, so that most of the time it is an anchor and a blessing—or a curse and a cross—depending on how we have chosen to approach it.

So many people search endlessly for "meaning" in their lives, often resisting the meaning that is right there. The point is not that we are lucky to have a child with a disability because it gives our lives instant meaning. The point is that to be presented with this event, and to fail to engage it as an opportunity—for focus, for meaning, for learning and growth, for a way to affect the world we live in—is to miss the experience that life has offered us. However, as Arnold Beisser points out in *Flying Without Wings,* "In order to see the opportunities, though, you must accept what happened *as if you have chosen it.*" (Emphasis added.)

Let me be thankful for this doorway to meaning. Let me have the courage to walk through it. Let me choose it now.

Standing on One Foot

To dispose a soul to action we must upset its equilibrium.

—ERIC HOFFER

To be balanced and steady physically is fairly easy for most of us if we are standing on two feet, the weight of our body distributed equally on each. When we really have to call on our ability to balance is when we are not on two feet. To ski downhill successfully we have to shift our weight from side to side. To dance ballet, ice skate, or perform the balance poses in yoga, we have to balance on one foot and move at the same time. Riding a bike also requires the ability to balance, to shift our weight instantaneously to maintain equilibrium and stay upright.

Physical balance gives us a way to better understand mental and emotional balance. No one's life script is limited to standing on two feet. Life delivers challenges and events to each of us that require us to shift our weight. One of our challenges is our child with a disability. Here is an event that stands us on one foot and demands that we move, that we change, to stay in balance.

If we are going to maintain our equilibrium as we respond to our child's needs, we've got to shift our weight. And as in biking, skiing, or assuming the tree pose, the more we practice, the more we do it, the better we get.

Second Wind

If you ever have a prolonged problem, do something that gives you something else to think about.

—OLIVE ANN BURNS

Changing our context—being with different people, in a different place, trying a different activity—is the way we refresh ourselves and free our minds from a persistent situation that threatens to claim all of our attention. Change gives us a second wind so that we can come back with new energy.

This is the principle behind vacations. But we can do a lot of things besides taking a trip that have the same effect. Sometimes it's as simple as dropping in at the Y for a pick-up ball game, catching a movie, or going to our job. It's a matter of doing something else that engages our full attention—something that has nothing to do with our problem.

Our child's disability and the ripples it sends through our family and our life present continuing challenges. We can't make our lives trouble-free, but we can change our context and rejuvenate ourselves.

Hate

You lose a lot of time hating people.

—MARIAN ANDERSON

I hate my husband for doing only what I ask him to do when it comes to what our child needs.

I hate my wife for having this baby, who has changed our life from what I had planned.

I hate my child's doctor for talking about him as if he weren't there.

I hate the neighborhood kids for teasing my daughter on the bus.

I hate my dad for avoiding us.

I hate my mother-in-law for pressing us to give our baby up for adoption.

I hate my ex-wife for being such a martyr.

I hate my ex-husband for leaving me alone with this child.

I hate my other children for being ashamed of their brother.

I hate my sister for always telling me what to do.

I hate my friend for being so impatient with my child.

I hate my son's teacher for patronizing me.

I hate my kid for his remoteness.

I hate myself for being so discouraged.

Although my emotion is very powerful and feels like hate, do I really hate these people? Do I hate my children, my partner, and myself? Isn't it more likely that I am angry at the situation I am in? Isn't it that I am in fact terribly disappointed and disillusioned at the way someone has behaved?

Today, I will imagine each of my hates is a balloon, and let go of it.

Grievance

"The horror of that moment," the King went on, "I shall never, never forget!"
"You will, though," the Queen said, "if you don't make a memorandum of it."

—LEWIS CARROLL

Affront, injustice, hurt, injury, distress—all fall under the category of grievance, and we have undoubtedly experienced every one of them several times over in our life with our child. When we remember the occasions of our grievances, the accompanying negative emotions can spring to life and be felt again, full-force. We vividly relive the dismay that engulfed us when we recall the doctor's recommendation that we institutionalize our baby, and choke again on the indignation we experienced when someone suggested that her disability was our fault.

It is easy to nurse grievances, to continually revisit them and relive negative emotions, but the habit of resentment is one that corrodes our spirit and embitters us. "The real danger is to get stuck in anger and resentment," writes Henri Nouwen in *Here and Now: Living in the Spirit.* "Then we start living as the 'wounded one,' always complaining that life isn't 'fair.' "

The wounds were real at the time, and it is inevitable and appropriate that we remember them. But to recall an event and remember that we were sad at the time is different from continually rehearsing the event in our mind and reliving the sadness. When we respond emotionally to past events, we block our perception of and emotional response to the present. We are like the proverbial broken record, stuck in one groove, endlessly repeating the same line. When we relive grievances, we can't move forward in our song.

Self-Reliance

Know when to tune out. If you listen to too much advice, you may wind up making other people's mistakes.

—ANN LANDERS

When you have a child with a disability, experts become a part of your life. Teachers, doctors, and various kinds of therapists and specialists are continually assessing your child and offering opinions and advice. We are grateful for the professionals whose skill and know-how help our kid eat, communicate, control violent impulses, ride a bike, learn to read, survive a shunt blockage, or suffer fewer seizures. At the same time any one of us can probably look back and identify the times when we ignored our instincts in favor of professional advice. We regret some of the decisions we made in our reliance on a professional.

In her book *Wake Me When It's Over*, the journalist Mary Kay Blakely tells the story of her brother Frank, a brilliant man who was severely manic-depressive and ultimately committed suicide. She speaks of participating in family therapy sessions when her brother was hospitalized and hearing a psychologist question and blame her mother for some of the ways she had cared for Frank when he was a baby, ways prescribed by her pediatrician. From her experience Mary Kay Blakely offers this conclusion: "Don't ever accept an expert's opinion if it violates your own, because the experts can change their minds. Ultimately, you stand alone, and your instincts are the only safe ground to stand upon. Only your own opinions will be defensible in court someday."

Let me have the courage and the responsibility to trust my instincts and make my own mistakes.

235

Parent Punishment

Outrage is the cover for humiliation—the last recourse of the powerless.

—ARNOLD BEISSER, WHO WAS PARALYZED BY POLIO
AT THE AGE OF TWENTY-FIVE

The practice of sending home excessive amounts of schoolwork for students with special needs is so widespread, and so resented by parents, that it has its own name: parent punishment. And parents truly do feel punished by the school's inability or refusal to adapt to the child's needs.

The problem became acute for a family whose son had attention deficit disorder the year he started middle school. Day after day, the child came home with hours of unfinished work. The parents told the teacher that the maximum amount of time they could reasonably spend every day was two hours—already more than district guidelines. Still, they were rarely able to finish what their child brought home.

One night the mother decided they would do it all, just to see how long it took. They ate an early supper and got right to work. Three hours later, when everything was finished, the mother sent her son to bed and headed into the kitchen, where the dirty supper dishes were stacked by the sink. Suddenly, looking at the congealed sauce and cold spaghetti, she became enraged. *The teacher was not solving the problem at school and was dumping it on her! Didn't she think they had a life? Why should a kid who already had to work twice as hard throughout the school day be expected to work double time at home, too? How dare the teacher ignore what they had been telling her!*

She sat down and wrote this note: *Dear Ms. Smith: We worked really hard. It took three hours, but we got all of the assignments fin-*

ished. Unfortunately we were unable to get to the enclosed, so I am sending it along to you. Thank you, Mary Jones. She found a box, packed in all the dirty dishes, taped the note to the top, and went to bed.

The next morning she reread the note, tore it up, and threw it in the wastebasket. She unpacked the dishes and put them in a pan of hot soapy water to soak. "Sarcasm," she thought to herself, "is the defense of the weak. I will not fight hostility with hostility." Then she called the local learning disabilities organization and spoke with an advocate, after which she called her son's case manager and scheduled a meeting to address the issue of homework.

Punishment is always humiliating, but when outrage drives our actions we are coming from a place where we feel powerless. We are not, in fact, powerless. Today, I will remember that the effective response to humiliation is the identification and use of my real power.

The Service System

But what I distrusted was meeting someone whose job it was to provide services when all they did was babble noncommittal generalizations or sugary phrases. I always ended up thinking, you're making a living off my sister, and our family, and others like us. And you're not giving us anything in return.

—MAUREEN LYNCH, WHOSE OLDER SISTER, MARY FRAN, HAS
DEVELOPMENTAL DISABILITIES DUE TO UNKNOWN CAUSES

Every person with a disability carries on her shoulders the weight of a hundred professionals—from the case worker to the physical therapist, from the special education teacher to the personal care attendant—who make their living from disability.

We parents often feel that weight on our own shoulders. There never seems to be one person to deal with, always a team. Who is accountable? Whom do you call, or call first? We have a front row seat at the Workings of Bureaucracy, making time every month for a useless visit from the home care agency, "because that's what the regulations require us to do." Every year we fill out a lengthy Medicaid application, even though nothing has changed, sending it off to a financial worker who has never met us but is intimately acquainted with our income and expenses.

We deal all the time with people who sincerely present themselves as helpers and caregivers, but who also have vested interests in their salary, their job security, and the politics of their workplace, interests that often conflict with our child's needs. As one father said when he challenged the decisions the school had made for his daughter, "The team meeting felt like the Inquisition. Nobody seemed to care what Susy needed. They were only thinking about how our requests were upsetting the bureaucratic apple cart. Everybody was protecting their own turf. It was incredible."

I didn't create the service system. I can't control it. I can control only my reactions and look for ways I can effectively influence the system. I can strive to resist blaming others, to avoid taking things personally, and to forgive the wrongs done me and my child so that I will have the strength to carry one hundred people on my back.

Discrepancy

But he hasn't got anything on!

—HANS CHRISTIAN ANDERSEN

There is a consistent and often a wide gap between the best ways to teach and care for children with disabilities and the actual practices used with them. As parents we are constantly being confronted with these discrepancies. We frequently discover that our children are being subjected to practices that are at worst abusive or illegal, and at best insensitive, misguided, or ineffective.

A father visits school and finds that his daughter, who cannot walk or speak, has not been taken to the toilet or changed when she soiled her pants. A mother discovers her adult daughter in tears when she arrives at her group home; her stuffed dog was taken away because new regulations say residents should have age-appropriate possessions. After the entire eighth-grade choir has taken its place standing on the risers, the parents of one singer watch in anguish as their daughter, all eyes focused on her alone, hobbles out on stage and sits in the specially placed chair.

These painful situations are all too common. Knowing how to deal with them is not always obvious and is never easy, especially when our objections concern the very people with whom we and our child have continuing relationships. Each time, we must go through a process of determining whether or not to speak up, whom to talk to, and what methods or strategies to use in raising our concern. The "Ten Tips for Effective Parent Advocacy" booklets don't begin to address the complexity of this process or help us resolve our intense feelings of outrage and frustration.

The world is not yet good enough for our children. Its emperors do not want to hear that they have nothing on. We have no choice but to live in the world as it is, suffering its discrepancies even as we work to bridge the gap.

Good Guys, Bad Guys

"Together We're Better"

—TITLE OF A MINNESOTA SCHOOL INCLUSION GRANT PROJECT

Ask any parent of a child with a disability to describe the most painful and negative experience he has had regarding his child, and the odds are very high that he will describe an encounter with a professional—probably a doctor or a teacher. Ask the same parent to name a person who made a crucial difference for his family and child, and he will again identify a professional.

Professionals constitute a significant portion of the cast in the drama of our life with our child, appearing in almost every scene and playing a multitude of roles. In their ranks we find our heroes and villains, allies and opponents, rescuers and persecutors, bitter enemies and beloved friends. These players exemplify the talented, creative, and compassionate, as well as the ignorant, cruel, and incompetent. Unfortunately, it is often the bad guys who play the leading roles in our memory.

Let's write a script for the good guys. It could star the pediatrician who hung in with us through house calls and emergency room visits, treating our baby's persistent, complicated health problems, or the excellent teacher who helped a child who once hated school become one who wanted to learn. It might feature the baby sitter whose loving enthusiasm for our child helped us overcome our own ambivalence. There will be key roles for the teacher who understood that the bad behavior was just a symptom; the case worker who took risks to get our child what he needed; the advocate who taught us to claim our rights; the prin-

242

cipal who praised our efforts; the minister whose support never wavered. It will be a musical, full of drama, laughter and tears, sorrows and triumphs, and it will end with a joyful song of praise and thanks.

Agents of Accountability

There is a shame in America. Countless human beings are suffering needlessly. Countless more families of these unfortunate victims of society's irresponsibility are in anguish, for they know, or suspect, the truth. Unwittingly, or unwillingly, they have been forced to institutionalize their loved one into a life of degradation and horror.

—BURTON BLATT AND FRED KAPLAN

Shine the light.

—ED ROBERTS

During World War II many men who were exempted from the military as religious conscientious objectors were assigned to alternative duty with Civilian Public Service teams and sent to work in state institutions for the mentally ill and retarded. They were horrified by the brutality and inhuman conditions of the institutions, and recorded instances in diaries and in letters to one another. After the war a group of them founded an organization to improve the institutions and began publishing articles in national magazines about their experiences. Their accounts were the first exposures in decades of the deplorable conditions in state institutions and an important contribution to eventual reform.

Three things about these men enabled them to speak out: they were "outsiders," with fresh, unbiased eyes, who got to see all the way inside; they had allies in one another who validated their perceptions and gave them the support of a group; they were men of conscience who refused to walk away from the suffering of other human beings. By recounting and by publicizing what they had seen, they acted according to their consciences and brought an unacceptable situation into public view.

Those of us who have a child with a disability become witnesses to the injustice and even suffering that is imposed on people with disabilities, and especially those with mental disabilities, by the very organizations that are charged with their care and instruction. As outsiders who get all the way inside, we are crucial agents of accountability. It is important that we keep our vision fresh and never become dulled to unacceptable realities, even though we cannot instantly or singlehandedly change them. It is important that we find allies, those who are seeing and naming what we are seeing and who share our purpose; it is vital that we "shine the light."

Activism

The personal is political.

—SLOGAN, WOMEN'S MOVEMENT OF THE 1970s

When our child came into our lives, we became part of a movement, although we probably did not know it at the time. Life for persons with disabilities has been revolutionized by the disability civil rights movement, and one of the major forces behind that movement is parents, especially mothers, of children with disabilities.

"Resistance," says Wilson Follett in his introduction to *Modern American Usage*, "always begins with individuals." Follett was talking about language, but the assertion applies equally to the parents of disabled children. We joined the movement the first time we said "No." No to our child having to live in a hospital, no to his being refused admission to school, no to a denial of medical benefits, no to separate classes, no to his being left off the team.

From acting solely on behalf of our own child, many of us have been drawn into broader political activism. Thousands of us work in paid or volunteer positions as lobbyists, advocates, and organizers. Others serve on school and governmental committees and task forces. Many disability organizations and networks were founded by parents and are headed by parents. Our ranks include those whose disability advocacy has led them to visible and influential positions in politics, education, and government. Some of us have raised legal challenges that resulted in changes for millions. The court cases that closed the doors of huge institutions and opened those of the public schools bear our names. But always the base of this pyramid of activists is composed of the tens of thousands of us, unseen and unsung, who write checks and letters and advocate every day in large and small ways for our own child.

No matter what our level of activity, whether we are part of an organized national group effort or are working alone in our neighborhood school to improve things for our own child, we are involved in a social and political process, and our advocacy has an impact.

Endurance

But I am afraid to look at my feelings now; afraid that I will discover that the emotions that have propelled me in the past will be gone and something worse will have taken their place: weariness . . . Can I last as long as it will take?

—VIRGINIA DELAND, WHOSE DAUGHTER, LISA,
HAS DEVELOPMENTAL DISABILITIES

Once we've undertaken a course of advocacy and political activism, on whatever level, we are confronted with another issue: endurance, our ability to stay the course. It is unlikely that we will have to fight only one or two battles for our child. On the contrary, it will be only occasionally that we can say we are completely satisfied with her situation. The enthusiasm we brought to issues when she was five may have faded by the time she is fifteen. And when we turn to the more global goals of full civil rights and a completely accessible society for persons with disabilities, there is far to go. On both the personal and the public front, it is a long road.

It is necessary to gauge our stamina and strength. Am I like the marathon runner who has the endurance to go long distances, pacing herself over the course? Or am I a sprinter, someone who can make a fast, all-out, explosive effort to achieve a specified goal? Maybe I am a relay runner; I can be in the race for a while, and then I need to pass the torch to another. Most of us become relay runners at one time or another because our demands at home are heavy. As relay runners, when we join or rejoin the race we need to remember to take the torch and learn from those who have come before us. We don't need to reinvent the wheel. And when we step out of the race, we need to pass the torch, sharing our knowledge and ideas with newcomers.

Above all, our assessment of what we can take on must be in accord with the larger goal of lasting.

History

But the important thing—we mustn't let our own failures of imagination tell us what must be the case in the universe.

—PATRICIA SMITH CHURCHLAND

Ideas have a history just as the human race and the earth each has a history. Sadly, the historical response to the lame, the halt, and the blind, to the idiot and the leper, is disheartening, a long record of exclusion and elimination. A single historical fact, like the origin of the word "idiot"—from the Greek *idios*, a private person or layman, connoting someone separate from public life—tells us much.

In the context of human history, the concept of a person with a disability as a fully entitled, self-defining individual is brand-new. It is so new that when we think about it we can easily feel skeptical and discouraged instead of convinced and optimistic. Our desire to believe this new reality is overshadowed by the dark pall of history. The past does not provide a tradition on which we can build, but a nightmare from which we must part.

We cannot be tethered by the dark past, but must be fueled into action by the outrage of it. We are like astronauts, jettisoning the booster rockets, shooting into deep, dark space, trusting that the moon is there, waiting for our arrival.

Diversity Experts

In demanding simple names for complex experiences, our society loses the precious details.

—JOHN HOCKENBERRY, PARAPLEGIC SINCE AN AUTO ACCIDENT
AT THE AGE OF NINETEEN

In her book *Mindfulness*, Ellen Langer describes an experiment she conducted with elementary school children to find out whether teaching them to be more aware of specific differences would reduce their tendency to stereotype people with handicaps. The children were shown slides of people with a variety of handicaps in diverse situations and were then asked questions about them. The exercises encouraged mindfulness by requiring the children to find several answers, not just *the* answer; to identify *how* problem situations might be solved, not just *whether* they could be solved; and to provide, not one, but several, explanations for a described situation. "Our results," writes Langer, "showed that children can be taught that handicaps are function-specific and not person-specific. Those given training in making mindful distinctions learned to be discriminating without prejudice."

The heightened awareness of difference that we have acquired by living with our child has taught us all these lessons. We know that disability is not an absolute, but depends on context; that all human skills and attributes lie along a spectrum; and that every person possesses some quality, ability, or lack of ability that deviates from the majority. We know, from experience in our family, how to reshape a social group to make space for all the different needs and wants. We are well equipped to show people how to be discriminating without prejudice, and our rapidly diversifying culture needs the mindfulness our experience has furnished. We can approach the world, saying, "This is the way it is with us. We're proud of who we are. This is what we have to offer."

Because our families are different, we can make a difference.

In-Jokes

*Only healthy people say that handicaps are not a fit subject for laughter:
they are a perfect subject for laughter; they are God's own banana peels.*

—WILFRED SHEED

Your daughter calls Taco Cabana, her favorite restaurant, Taco Banana.

There was a time when you knew your son was on the school bus if boots and lunch boxes were flying out the window as it went by.

You're at the mall with your daughter, and a little boy of about five comes up to the wheelchair. He stares solemnly for a full minute. "Are you a criminal?" he asks her.

Your son comes to supper, lays his action figure beside his plate, and says, "He's sleeping." Then he tips back his head, closes his eyes, and starts to snore.

You get into bed at night and feel cold, hard things with your toes, little metal cars stuffed way at the bottom of the bed by a child compelled to hide things in nooks and crannies and spaces and holes.

Your son has a full-time behavioral aide at school. Another child goes home and tells her parents, "A boy at school has a bodyguard."

Your daughter is home from school one day because her wheelchair is broken, and she keeps asking for your help with what she wants to do. You tell her she has to wait; you have work you need to do. "I need a larger staff!" she exclaims.

On an outing to the Grand Canyon your daughter expresses her full range of autistic sounds amidst all the tourists speaking English, Spanish, German, Japanese. A child approaches and asks, "What language is she speaking? I think it's Spanish. It's Spanish, isn't it?"

There are six messages on the answering machine from your adult son, calling from his group home. By the last one, his ability to say the letter *l* has given way before his frustration: "Where the he—, where the he—, where the he—, where the *fuck* is everybody," you hear.

There's a lot of funny stuff in our lives with our kids. Enjoy it!

Invisible Disability

Children and adolescents who have depression will never be candidates for a national disability poster.

—LILI FRANK GARFINKEL

Unlike kids whose disabilities are announced by their wheelchair or other physical features, many children have disabilities that are invisible, or that present themselves in ways society sees as negative and antisocial rather than as symptomatic of conditions that need treatment. The ordinary-looking child who begins to hit when thwarted is not immediately recognized by the uninformed observer as having a neurological disorder, but instead seems to be a "bad" boy. The sullen adolescent who won't answer when spoken to appears to others to be carrying teen defiance too far, since it is not obvious that his uncommunicativeness covers a life-threatening despair. In fact, these behaviors *are* symptomatic, and these children are as much in need of intervention and accommodation as the child with severe asthma or muscular dystrophy.

However, when the outward physical clues do not immediately signal "disability," the child tends to "pass" as a child who has no disability. His behavior is often seen as willful, malicious, or self-involved, and subject to being controlled. If the behavior is not controlled, punishment is seen as the appropriate response.

These children suffer greatly when their behavior is described as bad or undisciplined and when they are punished for behavior that arises out of their disability or out of inadequate or inappropriate responses to the disability. We likewise suffer when others refuse to understand that our child's behavior is an indication of a deeper problem, or when we are characterized as excusing or colluding in negative behavior.

Society should acknowledge the needs of all our children and give them equal value. We must embrace the children who frighten and alienate us, as well as the ones who warm our hearts.

Professional Parent

One subtle barrier to acquiring good information can be our social or professional role—that imposing persona we present to the world. In other words, who we are trying to be can get in the way of what we need to know.

—DANIEL GOLEMAN, PAUL KAUFMAN, AND MICHAEL RAY

Some of us were already working in a profession related to disability when we gave birth to or adopted a child with a disability, while many others of us took up work in the field as a result of our parenting experience. However we got there, a lot of us fill both roles, assuming a dual identity that has its special pitfalls.

When we identify strongly with our professional role, we may miss out as parents. We see ourselves as having the answers, so we quit asking questions. We don't think of going to a support group, because we're facilitating one. Focused on running our own project, we fail to ask what resources our agency has for our child. We may believe that revealing our own needs and problems will compromise our professional credibility. We never take the "Help me" stance, because we have assumed the "Let me help you" position.

We also can fall into certain traps that impair our effectiveness as professionals. One is believing that we must always have an answer. Another is thinking that our experience with our child is equivalent to that of other parents and the solutions that worked for us will work for them. We may even think we are qualified to speak for other parents, or adopt the belief that we always have to be "ahead" of the parents we serve, which leads us to discount or ignore what they say when it contradicts or is outside our expertise.

Although I have several personae, I am one person, and each of my roles inevitably informs the other. I am the kind of professional I am because I am a parent, and I am the kind of parent I am because I am a professional. Through open-mindedness and constant awareness, I will strive to bring the best of each role to the other.

Dancing

It seems to me that when it comes to things that are good for your body and your mind and your soul, dancing is right up there with prayer and laughter.

—PETER SCHICKELE, WHO HAD POLIO AS A BOY

A metropolitan newspaper asked readers who had been married over twenty years to write in and share what they thought had made their marriages last. One woman wrote that dancing was the crucial element. She and her husband had never quit dancing. They'd turn on the radio and boogie in the kitchen; when the kids came along, they danced as a family.

A radio show host told his listeners that his mother would play calypso music every Saturday morning as they all cleaned the house together. He had grown up, not to hate cleaning, but to love calypso. He couldn't vacuum without it!

The play *The Boys Next Door* depicts the lives of four men with developmental disabilities, one of whom has fallen in love. In one scene he appears with his girlfriend at a dance. Neither of them can dance very well; they are just sort of rocking back and forth. But through the use of fantasy sequence, the audience is permitted to see the couple as they see themselves. As an actress who played the girlfriend describes it, "the 'reality' of our inner lives is that we feel quite glamorous and capable and beautiful."

Dancing is fun. It's free. It is a universal physical language. And it makes us feel beautiful.

To Fight or Not to Fight

Still, the choice of pushing ahead through the obstacles or just going away was always a matter of selecting the lesser of two evils. Going away was always a defeat. Pushing ahead was never a victory . . .

—JOHN HOCKENBERRY

There are always obstacles, and there is always this choice: to push ahead or just go away, to fight or take the path of least resistance. One of the things that make the choice especially difficult is that we are often looking at what seems to be a lose-lose situation. Going away is a defeat. It always feels terrible, and doubly so because we have made the decision not for ourselves, but on behalf of our child. To compromise your own desires and best interests is one thing; to compromise those of your child is something else.

Almost worse is the realization that pushing ahead does not guarantee an unqualified victory. When you have to fight to get your kid somewhere, whether into the restaurant in his wheelchair, or into his neighborhood school with the other third-graders, or into the messenger job without a job coach, it is not uncommon to question whether you really want him to be there. Moreover, fighting back exacts a significant emotional toll. We feel a sense of injury and outrage in having to push at all, to have to make a case for a child's worth, to fight for what other children have automatically, to sue for what the law clearly states is his right. It seems a dubious success to secure a right for your child only to be shunned by your neighbors or the teachers at school. Even when we "win," it's never uncomplicated.

We will continue to face obstacles and we will continue to respond in different ways at different times. Sometimes we will go away, and sometimes we will push. The real wrong is that these choices must be made at all.

Letting People In

As you hold the pose, concentrate less on effort and more on opening—
make space between your muscles.

—YOGA INSTRUCTOR

Jean was talking on the phone to a former neighbor, eagerly answering the friendly, interested questions about the progress of her
seven-year-old son, who had mental disabilities. "You know,
Carol," she said, "this has been a month of breakthroughs. Tim is
dressing himself, he goes to sleep by himself, and just last night he
took a bath on his own." Carol was shocked. "I didn't realize you
were still having to do all those things," she told her friend.

Jean was startled by Carol's remark. She perceived herself as
being quite open about her son and his disability. But now she
realized that when she talked about her son, she tended to focus on
positive things. Certain details like her having to sit with him every
night to help him sleep never seemed to come up. She was working
so hard all the time that it never occurred to her that others did not
see her effort; that they only observed someone who was smoothly
handling all the challenges that came her way. She was like the
proverbial duck who appears to be floating serenely on the water
while paddling like hell underneath.

A lot of us are like Jean. We always try hard to do everything
asked of us and at the same time put on a cheerful face. We know
we need people's concern, but we do not want their pity. We're
afraid that if we show the daily details, pity will be the response.
We do not perceive how successfully we mask not only the daily
demands, but our pain, anger, anxiety, and fatigue. We do not see
that the image that fends off pity also shuts out empathy and help.

We shouldn't try so hard. We need to relax in who and what we are, to let people see our hard work *and* our vulnerability. We have to believe that there is a place between pity and heroic martyrdom, and that we will raise this child more effectively when we channel energy into creating openings in our lives for those who love us and our children.

Community

At its core the story is a declaration of dependence on community cooperation, just as the Ojibwa story is a declaration of dependence on the earth and its creatures.

—CHRISTOPHER VECSEY

Dependence has become almost a dirty word in our culture, and independence for persons with disabilities has become a much-cited goal. Yet healthy and appropriate dependence and interdependence are essential to human life and community, and in the name of independence, many people have been left bereft and alone.

When we think about our family, we must look not only at how our child depends on us and how we foster—or inhibit—her independence, but we must also look at how we depend on others to accomplish our task of raising this child.

Arnold Beisser, a psychiatrist whose legs were paralyzed by polio when he was twenty-five, eloquently explains the relationship between dependence and independence in his book *Flying Without Wings:* "Every living being depends on others of its kind and the environment for nourishment and support. So a feeling of independence is not based on a belief that one is self-sufficient, but on a confidence that what one needs *is* available from the outside. The wider the circle that we can rely upon, the more we can feel and behave independently."

The time may be right for a "declaration of dependence," for a move to identify and build circles of support for ourselves and for our child. Our children's extraordinary needs for support can serve as pathways to remind all of us of our dependence and of our need for relationships; they can be the catalyst for finding connection and community.

Holidays

If everybody was autistic, people would save a lot of money at Christmastime.

—SARAH, WHOSE BROTHER ISAAC IS AUTISTIC

A "holiday" means a day off from work, time away from school. Of course there is no day off from a disability, not for your child, not for you. Maybe that's why other people think holidays are sad times for families who have a child with a disability. Or maybe they assume that because holidays are times reserved for joyous festivities, and since we can no longer be joyful, the "happy holidays" are just painful reminders of what we're missing. But obviously neither of these premises is true: the holidays are not a time of unqualified happiness for anyone; and the presence of disability has not eliminated joy from our lives.

Certainly our child has changed our holidays, just as she's changed every other aspect of our lives. Some of those changes do make us sad, others make us happy, but most evoke the bittersweet compounds of pain and pleasure that characterize all complex human events and relationships.

The joy and excitement Elise's family feels the day she returns home for the holidays from the School for the Deaf is equaled only by the sad emptiness that overtakes them after she has gone back. For Aviva, her son Steve's inability to take food by mouth takes on extra poignancy at Chanukah, when he cannot stuff himself on latkes like the other children, but as she watches his unsteady hand light the tapers she also has a heightened awareness of the miracle of faith. The Browns are enthusiastic organizers of their town's July Fourth picnic, but they are resigned to leaving before the fireworks,

266

because Sophie can't tolerate the loud explosions. Gordon finds it hard to buy gifts for Eric, who never asks for much and has only a few interests. But every Christmas, when Eric is thrilled with each gift, even the new socks, Gordon knows that he has never seen such a pure example of the joy of giving and receiving.

As we alter our holiday rituals to accommodate our children with differences, we learn that although rituals help give a holiday structure and put its abstract meanings in concrete forms, they never contain the whole meaning of the holiday. Changing the ritual or having to do without the custom does not take the holiday away from us; it only opens other paths to that larger meaning.

Autonomy

Well-meant protectiveness gradually undermines any autonomy. And more coercive interference . . . defeats any shred of initiative.

—ELLEN LANGER

A father let his twelve-year-old with developmental disabilities walk to a neighbor's house on a cold winter day. On the way, the boy decided to visit a classmate and got lost several blocks from home. Another neighbor, who recognized him from school, saw him, asked him in, called his family, then brought him home. At first his parents felt embarrassed and guilty, afraid that their neighbors would think them irresponsible.

On reflection, they realized that their goals were being met. Their son was attending school with other kids in the neighborhood; people knew him. And because he was known, someone was there to help when things didn't work out right. Of course, they might not always be so lucky, but it was a risk worth taking, and their son was becoming a part of the community. He saw the neighborhood as *his* and had the idea he could go out into it.

In order to support our children's sense of autonomy and initiative, we must take risks and permit them to take risks. In order to take risks, we have to recognize and accept a level of dependence on the greater community.

Approval

My mom is great. She feels no excuses or explanations are necessary and takes him every and anywhere. The pride I cannot feel, she does.

—CATHY MCCLURE, WHOSE SON JOSHUA
HAS A PERVASIVE DEVELOPMENTAL DELAY

In *News from the Border: A Mother's Memoir of Her Autistic Son,* Jane McDonnell describes how, after a miserable year in a school, where the teacher had suggested her son's problems were the result of bad parenting, she took Paul, then three, for evaluation at a new, experimental school. Observing the testing through a one-way mirror, Jane saw how creative, patient, and kind the new teacher was. Later, the teacher met with Jane and was enthusiastic about Paul, commenting on his original learning style. "We stood in the hall with her for another few minutes, just enjoying the warmth of her company," McDonnell writes. "I felt an enormous relief seep into me. Here I was a good mother once again, and here Paul was an 'original,' not a freak. Best of all, here there was hope and understanding and warmth and respect for this different little boy."

We all need people who see us as good and competent parents, and who do not blame us for what is "wrong" and difficult about our child. We all need places to go where people can look past the fact that our child doesn't talk or doesn't respond to our directions. We need people who admire his physical beauty and his curiosity, or who recognize how clever he is in his mischief. We all need to go where our family is accepted as it is, and delight is taken in us and each of our children. And we all need people who show us the way, leading us by their example to the confidence or pride we have been struggling for. An ounce of this kind of love can offset a pound of criticism and hostility. In its presence we open like a day lily to the sun. If it isn't there, we have to find it. "Perhaps," writes Helen Featherstone, "getting comfort is a learned skill. We have to know where to go and how to describe our need. Otherwise we get hurt."

The day lily survives the night, closing its bloom, protecting itself until morning, when it again shows its fullness to the sun. We can protect ourselves and exist in the places where people deny our child and us the sun of their acceptance, approval, or praise. But we and our child must have sun. We must have people who shine on us, and places where we can relax, open, and grow.

Social Paradigms

I couldn't see how I would ever be able to reconcile the pleasure I took in our private experiences of nursing, rocking, and singing with the way the outside world viewed Aaron and our "tragedy." I felt trapped in other people's pictures, afraid I would never get free. He seemed like such a wonderful boy; I wanted people to look past his disability and see his soul inside.

—VICKIE NOBLE, WHOSE SON AARON HAS DOWN SYNDROME

To have a child with a disability is considered tragic, because a handicapping condition in America is considered a stigma. As Erving Goffman observes in his classic study of the subject, "By definition, of course, we believe the person with a stigma is not quite human." Obviously, having a child who is less than human can only be tragic.

This is the social construct our culture has devised vis-à-vis individuals with handicaps, and it is not easily relinquished. Never mind that a mother's actual experience of her baby is different from what society pictures it. Never mind that we parents *know* that the disability is not the whole child; *know* that the body, even the mind, are not the soul. People will work very hard to keep us fixed in their mind-sets, because to do otherwise is to give up deeply embedded social paradigms.

Trying to explain, saying, "No, no, you don't understand. It's not like that; it's like this," is to knock on the hard walls of preconceived ideas, walls that are not only rigid but extremely well defended. Often we will come away with a bloody hand, having had our experience denied, or distorted to fit the preconceived notion, or called something else—delusion, denial, false hope, fantasy.

We must reach deep within ourselves and out to one another to find the strength to hang on to our reality and insist on its truth in the face of mistaken or hostile social constructs. It took the Catholic Church almost four hundred years to admit that Galileo should not have been condemned as a heretic for proving that Copernicus was right about the sun. No matter what men believed, the sun never did revolve around the earth, and other people's ideas of our experience will never be the same as our experience.

Cuddlies

*Later, in an effort to get me to "accept Zach as he is," without compar-
ing him to other children and feeling the pain of what he can't do, Joe
asked, "Suppose there were three kinds of children instead of just two:
little girls, little boys, and little cuddlies."*

—FERN KUPFER, WHOSE SON ZACHARIAH WAS DIAGNOSED WITH A
DEGENERATIVE BRAIN DISORDER AT THE AGE OF THREE

Leslie and Marion, though not close friends, were acquaintances
who saw each other frequently because their young sons were
friends. When Marion became pregnant unexpectedly at forty-
three, Leslie, who had a son with Down syndrome, asked whether
she was going to have an amniocentesis. "No," said Marion.
"Whatever this baby is, is all right with us."

Leslie was deeply touched by Marion's answer and went home
feeling good about herself and her family, because Marion had
looked at her life close up and seen it as acceptable and possible, so
acceptable that, right next to the question of whether it would be a
boy or a girl, she had made room for the possibility that her baby
might have Down syndrome.

What if we quit saying to pregnant women, "Well, as long as it's
healthy." What if we dropped the phrase "She's a keeper!" What if,
in the house of expectations we build around unborn babies, there
was space for "cuddlies." What if we thought of every baby as a
keeper? How would that change what people saw as OK and liv-
able?

Raising the Floor

It's not how far we go. It's how we go far.

—YOGA INSTRUCTOR

Sometimes we have a very clear vision of what we want for our child, of how far we want to go. When that vision is innovative, even revolutionary, such as a truly inclusive society, it is doubtful that we can achieve it quickly. Dramatic social change depends not only on our own actions, but on bringing others along to a new way of thinking. State-of-the-art and cutting-edge solutions are not going to be quickly embraced and adopted by people comfortable with the status quo, and even when they are heralded, they are not going to be immediately and universally available. A parent committing himself to radical change is committing not to an outcome, but to a process of community discovery and awakening. How does one live every day with such high, such far-off goals?

When we feel frustrated with our inability to achieve our goals, we must focus on increasing the capacity to reach them, whether our own capacity or the capacity of the larger community. The beginning yoga student watches the teacher fold forward and grasp her feet in a perfect forward bend, and knows that he cannot possibly reach his feet. Nevertheless, he assumes the pose and does the best he can. As he pushes out his heels and uses his quadriceps to lift his kneecaps, he increases his ability to stretch his legs. As he pushes forward out of his pelvis, leading with his chest, he strengthens and stretches his back, thus moving infinitesimally closer to being able to lay his rib cage on his thighs. Every practice of the pose increases the student's capacity to do the pose, and the form of the pose itself provides the model for what he is moving toward.

Each movement is undertaken in accord with that model, so that his actions, even though they fall far short of the ideal pose, reveal intention and possess form and integrity.

We must strive to exercise the choices we have today in a way that is consistent with our vision, even when we know we will not achieve it soon or even in our lifetime. Our commitment will allow us to focus on the *how* instead of the *how far*, and enable us to move with confidence, satisfaction, and peace of mind toward that dreamed-of destination.

Our Other Children

Why is he famous? I'm the smart one.

—APRIL, FIVE, WHOSE BROTHER CHAD, TEN, IS PICTURED
ON POSTERS FOR THE LOCAL ARC

How do you explain to a very bright, pretty preschooler why so many people remember and exclaim over her older brother, who still doesn't know the alphabet, and don't seem to see her at all?

What do you suggest to a ten-year-old who reports that his sister is being teased on the bus by boys who are older and bigger than he is?

How can you satisfy your daughter's complaint that her brother gets to watch TV while she has to do chores?

How do you make up to two lovely, good girls for the fact that their brother has autographed photos of himself with the President, the First Lady, and Arnold Schwarzenegger, and they have never even been invited along?

Where do you find four hours a day *each* for your other two children to balance the four you spend on their sister's medical and hygiene routines?

How do you reassure and comfort an eleven-year-old who breaks down in sobs at the realization that his sister is going to be dependent on others, possibly on him, for her entire life?

How do you inculcate in a child a sense of tolerance, compassion, and responsibility for his brother, without placing adult burdens on his young shoulders?

How do you remain balanced about the talents and successes of your "normal" child when hers are the only ones you get to glory in?

How—and when—do you break it to your daughter that her brother's disability could be inherited by her sons?

When we have a child with extraordinary needs, our other children also have extraordinary needs. They need extra support to live with things they can't understand, and information and reassurance about their own physical and emotional health. They need us to listen especially carefully to their worries and concerns, and provide clear guidelines about what they are responsible for and what they are not. They deserve acknowledgment of their contradictory feelings and help in sorting out their dilemmas. They need explicit appreciation for their sacrifices and contributions.

Today, I will run a mental check to see whether, on balance, my expectations for each of my children are reasonable and whether each child in our family is getting most of what she needs most of the time. Today, I will hug all my children and tell them how important they are in this family.

Too Complicated

Vinetta sighed. Life was so complicated now. She had never reckoned on life being complicated. It was like knitting on a dozen different needles.

—SYLVIA WAUGH

Life with our kids is complicated. The disability itself is complicated. Our emotional responses are intense and contradictory. The medical issues are complex; the technology our children use is intricate. Filling out a medical assistance form is tricky, as is figuring out the special education system. Hunting for resources can be an experience in maze walking.

Then there are the multiple filters we have to run everything through. Our kid leaves for school happy and comes home irritable and belligerent. Is it physical: Is she constipated? Are her new shoes too tight? Or is it medical: Did we forget the medication today? Is she getting an ear infection? Or is it environmental: Did the teacher assign new seats? Is it frustration? Is she tired of not being understood when she speaks? Or is it just a mood, just being a kid.

Then of course there is all the rest of life—our other kids, our relationships, our job, what to have for supper, how to kill the crabgrass, when to take our vacation. We are knitting on at least a dozen needles. It is complicated and it is hard. But we do it. We drop a lot of stitches, but we knit our lives. And what interesting, varicolored, unique garments they turn out to be.

Touchstone

When I am too sad and too skinny to keep keeping, when I am a tiny thing against so many bricks, then it is I look at trees. When there is nothing left to look at on this street. Four who grew despite concrete. Four who reach and do not forget to reach. Four whose only reason is to be and be.

—SANDRA CISNEROS

On days when we are discouraged, when we begin to doubt our ability to endure, when we question the choices we have made and feel that the forces we are up against are insurmountable, we need something to contemplate that reminds us to remain rooted even as we strive. We may think about tall weeds, whose roots hold fast even as the wind presses their length flat to the ground. We may look at the stars, winking their message that the universe is old and vast and we are just one tiny part of it; the stars, telegraphing from a million years ago the news that our actions have limited consequences and the world does not depend upon us. We may invoke a prayer: *Grant me the serenity to accept the things I cannot change, the courage to change the things I can, and the wisdom to know the difference.*

We need one constant thing to turn to for the reminder that we can endure and grow in the place we occupy.

Pearl

The food, her vigilance—this is what she can give to him. This is what she has always given to him. And he, lying there, though inert, gives back to her in return the dailiness of their lives—that which gives love its openings.

—SUE HALPERN DESCRIBING A MOTHER'S WATCH
OVER HER ADULT SON WHO IS DYING OF AIDS

We give what we can, and our child gives back to us the dailiness of our life, the simple, regular, and repeated interactions and activities that anchor and ground our existence. Every day we stretch her contracted muscles. We feed her, give the medications, turn and reposition her, bathe, massage, and hold her. Comb her hair. Like nacre building around the grain of sand in the oyster's shell, the dailiness of our lives accrues, until one day there is a pearl, the love we have been opened to.

Death

There is no way to predict how you will feel.

—EARL A. GROLLMAN

If you live in a place where winter is lengthy and harsh, you know that each year you never quite believe in its severity until it arrives. Through the autumn, even though frost has killed the garden and the gray, rainy days increase, you think of the cold days as exceptions to the sunny ones that still predominate. Just when you are about to get out the heavy coats, the weather turns warm again, and you don't bother. And then one day winter bites down hard. The wind blows so bitterly you sense the size of the beast behind it; he is close, and not just on an exploratory prowl, but hunkered down for good. That day, which comes as a shock, is the day you start to believe in this particular winter.

We can know certain things are going to happen and still be surprised by them when they occur. The inevitable is not real until it actually happens. It takes an incarnation: the idea, the concept, the word has to take on flesh and we have to know it through our senses to be able to experience it. Our child's death, which we know will be early, and which perhaps we have come right up to many times, will be like that: a familiar and expected idea that surprises us when it happens. Then we will know that we could not have believed it before. We will know that there was no way we could have been ready.

Transformation

Only the broken heart has the ghost of a chance to grieve, to forgive, to long, to transform.

—CHRISTINA BALDWIN

You run into a couple you know, their three- and five-year-olds in tow. "We just got back from vacation," they say, grinning widely. "It's the first time we've been on vacation as a family." It has been two years since their son, overwhelmed by his many severe disabilities, died at the age of seven.

Another mother announces, "I hardly know what to do with my time." This is the first year her daughter, Amy, hasn't missed a day of school since she started attending a special early-childhood program when she was eighteen months old. Amy is now fifteen.

At Christmas you receive a card from a couple you know whose son cannot walk or speak. Inside is a photo of Morgan and his two brothers. He is ten and breathtakingly handsome, but his parents have no idea what kind of mind is working behind this boy's beautiful face. It is the first year they have sent Christmas cards since Morgan was diagnosed with muscular dystrophy eight years ago.

Maybe these people are friends of ours. Maybe they are us. We hear them, or we hear ourselves saying the same things. We think about what it means not to take a vacation in nine years, not to be able to take your family on a trip together; what it means to deal with illness and missed days of school and upset schedules for fifteen years; what it means to feel so overwhelmed, or depressed, or cut off from the joy of life, that you can no longer participate in Christmas or the other rituals that bind people together. In these moments we realize the huge impact this disability has had on our lives. We feel the losses it has imposed, the price it has exacted.

I will feel and honor my loss and my grief; I will allow forgiveness and attend to my longing; I will measure and know my strength. I will celebrate the transformation wrought in me.

God

Wherever you turn is God's face.

—MUHAMMAD

The father of Ben, a boy with Down syndrome, was attending a family funeral when the minister quoted Meister Eckhart's comment that God is like someone hiding who coughs to give himself away. Memories of hide-and-seek games with Ben immediately flashed into the father's mind. Though he was sixteen years old, Ben had not lost his love for this game and often invited visitors to play with him, sometimes to the embarrassment of his family. He hid brilliantly, but always gave himself away with a wonderful chuckle. The seeker would be in the basement storeroom, or looking between coats in the closet, and from another part of the room, there it would come, the most delightful, delighted throaty laugh. You were so close, he couldn't bear it if you didn't find him.

"Wow," thought the father, filled with wonder and awe, his heart flooding with love for his son, *"that's* what God is like."

Beautiful

I often tell Walter someday he will talk to Daddy. We have our own private sign for this. He touches his forehead with his forefingers and I touch my chest. I say I know the words in his mind will come to my heart. I say "Daddy knows."

—RICHARD C. ANDERSON, whose son Walter is autistic

Do you know how beautiful you are? You are! You are! I see your tenderness, your unqualified love, your patience and dedication. I see your wounded pride, your doubt, anxiety, and rage. I see you adjusted to life as it is and tortured by impossible choices. I see you enlarged and compromised. I see all of you, and always, I see how beautiful you are.

Resources

The first and most important thing for parents to know is that there is a huge array of programs and services for children with disabilities and their families. At a minimum, every family should be aware that their child is entitled by law to a free and appropriate public education. Even a partial list of the additional services one can obtain, often free or at reduced cost, would include: legal advice and advocacy, medical insurance and services, in-home assistance, specialized equipment, respite care, social and recreational activities, access to parent networks, and family counseling. For almost any need that arises relative to their child with a disability, families should at least ask themselves, "Where can we get help with this?"

While it is vital for families to be aware of specialized disability services, these do not represent the only source of support. I would encourage parents looking for help to begin close to home. Explore the resources in the web of communities to which you already belong: your own family, your church, your neighborhood and city. Don't assume that you need specialized services or specially trained people or special programs to meet your child's and your own needs. Think generically, and ask what is available in the community for children the same age as yours. Other families of young children need baby sitters and day care, too. Where do they find them? Can that work for you? Everyone needs exercise. What is there at the local Y or your health club that interests your child? Millions of people have found support in twelve-step programs for living with difficult realities. You can, too. In short, don't rule yourself or your child out of regular life. It will work for you far more than you might ever imagine.

Everyone has his or her own style of gathering information. Some of us go right to the library or our computer and conduct a systematic search. Others of us just start asking around. Often we do some of both. Once again, the easiest way to begin finding what you need might be to start close to home and with what is ready-to-hand, using the same methods that work for you in other situations. Network the way you would if you were looking for a job or a plumber. Talk to the professionals who are involved with your child—the teachers, doctors, and social workers. Talk to your neighbors, co-workers, friends, and family. Search out other parents. No one's situation or needs will be exactly like yours, but people who have lived with a certain disability for many years are going to be rich with information, and veterans of the service system can be your best guide to it. You may be feeling incredibly alone with your problem, but millions of children and adults have disabilities. They and their friends and relatives are all around you, and will lead you to new information or possibilities. A look in the phone book and a trip to the library or on the Internet will provide more leads than you can follow in one day.

The following organizations are the primary sources of disability services:

Government agencies. Government agencies are a key source of services for children and families, either directly providing or funding those services required by law. For example, federal law requires schools to educate all children with disabilities, and all states must provide some level of services for children beginning at birth. Every city, county, and state will offer some level of service and information. Look in the blue government pages of the phone book. Logical departments are education, health, social or human services, or children and family services. You may make a lot of calls and be bounced around a bit, but with persistence you will be able to determine what government services are available for your child, and where and how to apply for them.

Disability organizations. There are scores of private, nonprofit agencies dedicated to disability in general or to a specific disability, for example, the Down Syndrome Congress, United Cerebral Palsy, the National Organization for Rare Disorders, the Disability Rights Education and Defense Fund, World Institute on Disability. Many of these agencies have national, state, and local chapters. Disability agencies typically provide information and referral services—they can tell you where to go to find the service you are looking for; they conduct training workshops and conferences on topics ranging from education to sexuality; they undertake advocacy—they are knowledgeable about disability legislation, engage in lobbying, and can also provide individual advocates to help parents negotiate with their county or school district. These agencies often sponsor support groups, and some operate specialized services, such as respite care programs, social activities, or camps.

Legal Aid Society. Every state is required by federal law to have a protection and advocacy agency for persons with disabilities. In most states the Legal Aid Society has this responsibility, and provides legal information, advice, and representation free of charge.

Major universities are often home to research institutes, experts, and programs devoted to certain disabilities or disability-related topics.

Churches, private philanthropic organizations, and private hospitals, especially children's hospitals, may offer certain services specifically related to disability.

Generic organizations. Groups like the YMCA and the Boy

Scouts and Girl Scouts, as well as community playground and park and recreation departments, are increasingly committed to serving all children, including children with disabilities.

The world of disability services is far from ideal. Its very size and complexity make it hard to understand and use and it is filled with gaps, overlaps, and glitches. In most cases it will not reach out and touch *you; you* will have to tackle it. It will not always yield exactly what you need or everything you need. But if you are creative and persistent, if you can accept the haphazard, serendipitous, time-consuming nature of the process, and realize that you are going to become your own expert, then you will go out into your community and the specialized universe of disability service systems and find solutions that work for you, your child, and your family.

Source Notes

PART ONE

p. 11   John McPhee, *Basin and Range* (New York: Farrar, Straus & Giroux, 1981), p. 25.

p. 15   Rosalie Maggio, comp., *The Beacon Book of Quotations by Women* (Boston: Beacon Press, 1992), p. 28.

p. 16   Anchee Min, *Red Azalea* (New York: Pantheon Books, 1994), p. 193.

p. 17   L. Tobin, *What Do You Do With a Child Like This? Inside the Lives of Troubled Children* (Duluth, MN: Whole Person Associates, 1991), p. 146.

p. 18   C. S. Lewis, *A Grief Observed* (London: Faber & Faber, 1961; New York: Bantam Books, 1976), p. 1 (page citation is to the reprint edition).

p. 20   Harold S. Kushner, *When Bad Things Happen to Good People* (New York: Schocken Books, 1981; New York: Avon Books, 1983), p. 46 (page citation is to the reprint edition).

p. 21   Elisabeth Kübler-Ross, *On Death and Dying* (New York: Macmillan, 1969; New York: Collier Books, 1993), p. 4 (page citation is to the reprint edition).
Josh Greenfeld, *A Place for Noah* (New York: Henry Holt, 1978; San Diego: Harcourt Brace Jovanovich, 1988), p. 4 (page citation is to the reprint edition).

p. 22   Ellen Pall, "Painting Life into Sammy," *New York Times Magazine,* 29 January 1995, pp. 38–39.

p. 23   Annie Dillard, *Holy the Firm* (New York: Harper & Row, 1977; New York: Perennial Library, 1988), p. 11 (page citation is to the reprint edition).

E. B. White, *Stuart Little* (New York: Harper & Row, 1945; New York: Harper Trophy, 1973), pp. 92–93 (page citations are to the reprint edition).

p. 24   Rosalie Maggio, comp., *The Beacon Book of Quotations by Women* (Boston: Beacon Press, 1992), p. 302.

p. 25   Anne Lamott, *Bird by Bird: Some Instructions on Writing and Life* (New York: Pantheon Books, 1994), p. 18.

p. 26   Sylvia Waugh, *The Mennyms* (New York: Greenwillow Books, 1993), p. 158.

p. 28   Marsha Forest and John O'Brien, *Action for Inclusion: How to Improve Schools by Welcoming Children with Special Needs into Regular Classrooms* (Toronto: Inclusion Press, 1989), p. 3.

p. 29   Leah Cohen, *Train Go Sorry: Inside a Deaf World* (New York: Houghton Mifflin, 1994; New York: Vintage Books, 1995), p. 295 (page citation is to the reprint edition).

p. 30   Madeleine L'Engle, *A Wrinkle in Time* (New York: Farrar, Straus & Giroux, 1962), p. 154.

p. 32   Fred Rogers, *You Are Special: Words of Wisdom from America's Most Beloved Neighbor* (New York: Viking, 1994), p. 6.
Oliver Sacks, *The Man Who Mistook His Wife for a Hat* (New York: Summit Books, 1985), pp. 171–72, 173.

p. 34   Benjamin Hoff, *The Te of Piglet* (New York: E. P. Dutton, 1992; New York: Penguin Books, 1993), p. 183 (page citation is to the reprint edition).

p. 35   Lauri Klobas, "A Few Words from Rift Fournier," *The Disability Rag,* May-June 1989, p. 4.

p. 36   Quoted in Erving Goffman, *Stigma: Notes on the Management of Spoiled Identity* (New York: Simon & Schuster, 1963; New York: Touchstone, 1986), p. 35.

p. 38   Lawrence Van Gelder, "Victor Reisel, 81, Columnist Blinded by Acid Attack, Dies," *New York Times,* 5 January 1995, sec. B, p. 11.

p. 39   A. A. Milne, *The World of Pooh: The Complete Winnie-the-Pooh and The House at Pooh Corners* (New York: E. P. Dutton, 1957), p. 12.

Justin Kaplan, ed., *Bartlett's Familiar Quotations* (Boston: Little, Brown & Co., 1992), p. 528:15.

p. 40 Jane Taylor McDonnell, *News from the Border: A Mother's Memoir of Her Autistic Son* (New York: Ticknor & Fields, 1993), p. 14.

p. 41 Tom Sullivan, *Special Parent, Special Child: Parents of Children with Disabilities Share Their Trials, Triumphs, and Hard-Won Wisdom* (New York: G. P. Putnam's Sons, 1995), p. 28.

p. 42 Larry Woiwode, *Beyond the Bedroom Wall* (New York: Farrar, Straus & Giroux, 1975), p. 203.

p. 43 Mary Pielaet, "Untold Diagnosis," in *Making Changes: Family Voices on Living with Disability* (New York: Harcourt Brace Jovanovich, 1987), p. 30.

p. 47 Charles R. Callanan, *Since Owen: A Parent-to-Parent Guide for Care of the Disabled Child* (Baltimore: Johns Hopkins University Press, 1990), p. 149.

p. 49 Curt Meine, *Aldo Leopold: His Life and Work* (Madison, WI: University of Wisconsin Press, 1988), p. 252.

p. 51 E. B. White, "Here Is New York," *Essays of E. B. White* (New York: HarperCollins, 1977; New York: Harper Colophon, 1979), p. 131 (page citation is to the reprint edition).

p. 52 Josh Greenfeld, *A Place for Noah* (New York: Henry Holt, 1978; San Diego: Harcourt Brace Jovanovich, 1988), p. 64 (page citation is to the reprint edition).

p. 54 Elisabeth Kübler-Ross, *On Death and Dying* (New York: Macmillan, 1969; New York: Collier Books, 1993), p. 123 (page citation is to the reprint edition).

p. 57 Helen Featherstone, *A Difference in the Family: Living with a Disabled Child* (New York: Basic Books, 1980; New York: Penguin Books, 1981), p. 100 (page citation is to the reprint edition).

p. 59 Justin Kaplan, ed., *Bartlett's Familiar Quotations* (Boston: Little, Brown & Co., 1992), p. 546:3.

p. 61 "Jonas Salk, Whose Vaccine Stopped Polio, Dies at 80," *Minneapolis StarTribune,* 24 June 1995, p. 1.

p. 63 Benjamin Hoff, *The Tao of Pooh* (New York: E. P. Dutton, 1982;

New York: Penguin Books, 1983), pp. 57–58 (page citations are to the reprint edition).

p. 64   Lucy Gwin, "How It's S'posed to Be—An Interview with Ed Roberts," *Mouth: The Voice of Disability Rights*, July 1992, p. 23.

p. 65   Rosalie Maggio, comp., *The Beacon Book of Quotations by Women* (Boston: Beacon Press, 1992), p. 129.

p. 67   Chip Brown, "The Visit," *Self*, February 1989, p. 138.

p. 69   Justin Kaplan, ed., *Bartlett's Familiar Quotations* (Boston: Little, Brown & Co., 1992), p. 684:17.

p. 71   Arnold Beisser, *The Only Gift: Thoughts on the Meaning of Friends and Friendship* (New York: Doubleday, 1991), p. 146.

p. 72   Rosalie Maggio, comp., *The Beacon Book of Quotations by Women* (Boston: Beacon Press, 1992), p. 133.

p. 73   A. A. Milne, *The World of Pooh: The Complete Winnie-the-Pooh and The House at Pooh Corners* (New York: E. P. Dutton, 1957), p. 291.

p. 76   Joseph P. Shapiro, *No Pity: People with Disabilities Forging a New Civil Rights Movement* (New York: Times Books, 1993), p. 3.

p. 77   Helle Mittler, *Families Speak Out: International Perspectives on Families' Experiences of Disability* (Cambridge, MA: Brookline Books, 1995), p. 81.

p. 78   Charles R. Callanan, *Since Owen: A Parent-to-Parent Guide for Care of the Disabled Child* (Baltimore: Johns Hopkins University Press, 1990), p. 4.
Alex Witchell, "Placing the Person Ahead of the Crown," *New York Times,* 17 October 1994, sec. B, p. 1.

p. 80   Vivian Gussin Paley, *You Can't Say You Can't Play* (Cambridge, MA: Harvard University Press, 1992; Cambridge, MA: Harvard University Press Paperback, 1993), pp. 103, 33 (page citations are to the reprint edition).

p. 81   Michael Bérubé, "A Father, a Son, and Genetic Destiny," *Harper's*, December 1994, p. 43.

p. 84   Tama Starr, comp., *The "Natural" Inferiority of Women: Outrageous Pronouncements by Misguided Males* (New York: Poseidon Press, 1991), p. 32.

Carol Gilligan, *In a Different Voice: Psychological Theory and Women's Development* (Cambridge, MA: Harvard University Press, 1982), pp. 6, 14.

p. 86   Susanna Kaysen, *Girl, Interrupted* (New York: Random House, 1993; New York: Vintage Books, 1994), p. 5 (page citation is to the reprint edition).

p. 87   Rainer Maria Rilke, *Letters to a Young Poet,* rev. ed., trans. M. D. Herter Norton (New York: W. W. Norton, 1954; Norton Paperback, 1993), p. 34 (page citation is to the reprint edition).

p. 88   Melba Colgrove, Harold H. Bloomfield, and Peter McWilliams, *How to Survive the Loss of a Love* (Santa Monica: Prelude Press, 1991), p. 180.

p. 90   Justin Kaplan, ed., *Bartlett's Familiar Quotations* (Boston: Little, Brown & Co., 1992), p. 527:27.

p. 91   Jayne D. B. Marsh, ed., *From the Heart: On Being the Mother of a Child with Special Needs* (Bethesda, MD: Woodbine House, 1995), p. 84.

p. 93   Larry Woiwode, *Beyond the Bedroom Wall* (New York: Farrar, Straus & Giroux), 1975, p. 203.

p. 94   Fern Kupfer, *Before and After Zachariah: A True Story about a Family and a Different Kind of Courage* (New York: Delacorte Press, 1982; Chicago: Academy Chicago Publishers, 1982), p. xiii (page citation is to the reprint edition).

p. 96   David Seerman, "The Loneliness of the Long-Distance Daddy," in Donald J. Meyer, ed., *Uncommon Fathers: Reflections on Raising a Child with a Disability* (Bethesda, MD: Woodbine House, 1995), p. 89.

p. 97   Helen Featherstone, *A Difference in the Family: Living with a Disabled Child* (New York: Basic Books, 1980; New York: Penguin Books, 1981), pp. 83–84 (page citations are to the reprint edition).

p. 98   Thomas Merton, *Conjectures of a Guilty Bystander* (Garden City, NY: Doubleday, 1966; New York: Image Books, 1989), p. 158 (page citation is to the reprint edition).

p. 99   John McPhee, *Rising from the Plains* (New York: Farrar, Straus & Giroux, 1986), p. 65.

PART TWO

p. 101   Clara Claiborne Park, *The Siege: The First Eight Years of an Autistic Child* (Boston: Little, Brown & Co., 1982), p. 196.

p. 103   Ellen Langer, *Mindfulness* (Reading, MA: Addison-Wesley, 1989; Reading, MA: Addison-Wesley Paperback, 1990), p. 192 (page citation is to the reprint edition).

p. 105   Erma Bombeck, *I Want to Grow Hair, I Want to Grow Up, I Want to Go to Boise: Children Surviving Cancer* (New York: Harper & Row, 1989), p. 63.

p. 106   Claudia Dreifus, "Chloe Wofford Talks About Toni Morrison," *New York Times Magazine*, 11 September 1994, p. 74.

p. 109   Rainer Maria Rilke, *Letters to a Young Poet*, rev. ed., trans. M. D. Herter Norton (New York: W. W. Norton, 1954; Norton Paperback, 1993), p. 23 (page citation is to the reprint edition).

p. 111   Justin Kaplan, ed., *Bartlett's Familiar Quotations* (Boston: Little, Brown & Co., 1992), p. 546:9.

p. 114   Michael Ondaatje, *The English Patient* (New York: Alfred A. Knopf, 1992; New York: Vintage Books, 1993), p. 199 (page citation is to the reprint edition).

p. 115   David Dawson and Jean Edwards, *My Friend David: A Source Book about Down Syndrome and a Personal Story about Friendship* (Portland, OR: EDNICK Communications, 1983), p. 39.

p. 117   Fred Rogers, *You Are Special: Words of Wisdom from America's Most Beloved Neighbor* (New York: Viking, 1994), p. 39.
         D. Patrick Miller, *A Little Book of Forgiveness* (New York: Viking, 1994), p. 75.

p. 118   Gretchen B. Dianda and Betty J. Hofmayer, eds., *Older and Wiser: 716 Memorable Quotes from Those Who Have Lived the Longest and Seen the Most* (New York: Ballantine Books, 1995), p. 162.

p. 119   Josh Greenfeld, *A Child Called Noah* (New York: Henry Holt,

1972; San Diego: Harcourt Brace Jovanovich, 1988), p. 139 (page citation is to the reprint edition).

p. 121 Wilfred Sheed, *In Love with Daylight: A Memoir of Recovery* (New York: Simon & Schuster, 1995), p. 27.

p. 123 Brie Quinby, "Be Glad You're Not a Perfect Mother," *Woman's Day,* 17 January 1989, p. 86.

p. 125 Louise Erdrich, *The Bingo Palace* (New York: HarperCollins, 1994), p. 226.

p. 129 Lynette Shaw, "Why I Fight for Mainstreaming," *Minneapolis StarTribune,* 2 April 1995, sec. A, p. 25.

p. 130 Michael Dorris, *Paper Trail: Essays* (New York: HarperCollins, 1994; New York: Harper Perennial Edition, 1995), p. 115 (page citation is to the reprint edition).

p. 132 Clara Claiborne Park, *The Siege: The First Eight Years of an Autistic Child* (Little, Brown & Co., 1982), p. 50.

p. 133 Jason Kingsley and Mitchell Levitz, *Count Us In: Growing Up with Down Syndrome* (New York: Harcourt Brace, 1994), p. 44.

p. 135 Rosalie Maggio, comp., *The Beacon Book of Quotations by Women* (Boston: Beacon Press, 1992), p. 116.

p. 136 Madeleine L'Engle, *Walking on Water: Reflections on Faith and Art* (Wheaton, IL: Harold Shaw Publishers, 1980), p. 114.

p. 137 Alan Bennett, *Writing Home* (New York: Random House, 1994), pp. 137–38.
        Louise Erdrich, foreword to *The Broken Cord,* by Michael Dorris (New York: Harper & Row, 1989; New York: Harper Perennial, 1990), p. xii (page citation is to the reprint edition).

p. 138 Temple Grandin, *Thinking in Pictures* (New York: Doubleday, 1995), p. 99.

p. 139 Christina Baldwin, *Life's Companion: Journal Writing as a Spiritual Quest* (New York: Bantam Books, 1991), pp. 227–29.

p. 141 Tom Waits, *Frank's Wild Years,* sound recording, Island 842357.

p. 145 Susanna Kaysen, *Girl, Interrupted* (New York: Random House, 1993; New York: Vintage Books, 1994), p. 84 (page citation is to the reprint edition).

p. 146 Louise Erdrich, foreword to *The Broken Cord,* by Michael Dorris

(New York: Harper & Row, 1989; New York: Harper Perennial, 1990), p. xv (page citation is to the reprint edition).

p. 147   Madeleine L'Engle, *Walking on Water: Reflections on Faith and Art* (Wheaton, IL: Harold Shaw Publishers, 1980), p. 61.

p. 148   Joseph P. Shapiro, *No Pity: People with Disabilities Forging a New Civil Rights Movement* (New York: Times Books, 1993), p. 149.

p. 149   Benjamin Hoff, *The Te of Piglet* (New York: E. P. Dutton, 1992; New York: Penguin Books, 1993), pp. 169, 170–71 (page citations are to the reprint edition).

p. 151   Lewis Carroll, *Through the Looking-Glass* (New York: William Morrow, 1992), p. 204.

p. 153   Rosalie Maggio, comp., *The Beacon Book of Quotations by Women* (Boston: Beacon Press, 1992), p. 273.

p. 155   Arnold Beisser, *The Only Gift: Thoughts on the Meaning of Friends and Friendship* (New York: Doubleday, 1991), p. 118.

p. 156   Robin Simons, *After the Tears: Parents Talk about Raising a Child with a Disability* (New York: Harcourt Brace Jovanovich, 1987), p. 54.

p. 157   Mary Pielaet, "Untold Diagnosis," in *Making Changes: Family Voices on Living with Disability,* Jan A. Spiegle and Richard A. van den Pol, eds. (Cambridge, MA: Brookline Books, 1993), p. 41.

p. 159   Emily Dickinson, #365, *The Complete Poems of Emily Dickinson,* Thomas H. Jackson, ed. (Boston: Little, Brown & Co., 1960), p. 173.

p. 161   Franklin D. Roosevelt, Inaugural Address, March 4, 1933, in *The Public Papers and Addresses of Franklin D. Roosevelt,* vol. II, comp. Samuel Rosemman (New York: Russell & Russell, 1933), p. 11.

p. 162   Andie Tucher, ed., *Bill Moyers: World of Ideas II* (New York: Doubleday, 1990), p. 147.

p. 163   E. B. White, *Stuart Little* (New York: Harper & Row, 1945; New York: Harper Trophy Book, 1973), p. 9 (page citation is to the reprint edition).

p. 165   Dorothy Winbush Riley, ed., *My Soul Looks Back, 'Less I Forget: A Collection of Quotations by People of Color* (New York: HarperCollins Publishers, 1993), p. 221.

p. 167   Louis Simpson, "Shattering Germany," *New York Times Magazine*, 7 May 1995, p. 77.

p. 168   John Callahan, *Don't Worry, He Won't Get Far on Foot: The Autobiography of a Dangerous Man* (New York: William Morrow, 1989), p. 216.

p. 169   Sue Halpern, *Migrations to Solitude* (New York: Pantheon Books, 1992), p. 144.

p. 170   Phyllis Root, "Telling Stories," *A View from the Loft: A Magazine about Writing*, June 1995, p. 20.

p. 172   Temple Grandin, in a speech to the Twin Cities Autism Society, May 15, 1994. Ms. Grandin makes this point in slightly different words in her book *Thinking in Pictures: And Other Reports from My Life with Autism* (New York: Doubleday, 1995), p. 80.

p. 174   "Bein' Green," words and music by Joe Raposo.

p. 175   Ben Adams, "Our Brave New World," in *Uncommon Fathers: Reflections on Raising a Child with a Disability*, Donald J. Meyer, ed. (Bethesda, MD: Woodbine House, 1995), p. 55.

p. 176   Vivian Gussin Paley, *The Boy Who Would Be a Helicopter: The Uses of Storytelling in the Classroom* (Cambridge, MA: Harvard University Press, 1990; Cambridge, MA: Harvard University Press Paperback, 1991), pp. 1, 99–100 (page citations are to the reprint edition).

p. 178   Michael Dorris, *The Broken Cord* (New York: Harper & Row, 1989; New York: Harper Perennial, 1990), p. 200 (page citation is to the reprint edition).

p. 182   Sue Halpern, *Migrations to Solitude* (New York: Pantheon Books, 1992), pp. 13–14.

p. 184   Justin Kaplan, ed., *Bartlett's Familiar Quotations* (Boston: Little, Brown & Co., 1992), p. 398, n. 1.

p. 186   Laurence J. Peters, ed., *Peters' Quotations: Ideas for Our Time* (New York: William Morrow, 1977), p. 302.
         Justin Kaplan, ed., *Bartlett's Familiar Quotations* (Boston: Little, Brown & Co., 1992), p. 754:14.

p. 187   Ellen Langer, *Mindfulness* (Reading, MA: Addison-Wesley Pub-

lishing Company, 1989; Reading, MA: Addison-Wesley Paperback, 1990), p. 143 (page citation is to the reprint edition).

p. 189   Rosalie Maggio, comp., *The Beacon Book of Quotations by Women*
(Boston: Beacon Press, 1992), p. 301.

p. 191   William Safire and Leonard Safir, comps. and eds., *Words of Wisdom: More Good Advice* (New York: Simon & Schuster, 1989), p.
249.
Dr. Seuss, *The Cat in the Hat* (New York: Random House, 1985),
p. 18.

p. 194   Sherokee Ilse, *Precious Lives, Painful Choices: A Prenatal Decision-
making Guide* (Long Lake, MN: Wintergreen Press, 1993), p. 6.

p. 196   Laura Ingalls Wilder, *The Long Winter* (New York: Harper &
Row, 1940; New York: Scholastic Books, 1968), pp. 310–11
(page citations are to the reprint edition).

p. 197   Melba Colgrove, Harold Bloomfield, and Peter McWilliams, *How
to Survive the Loss of a Love* (Santa Monica: Prelude Press, 1991),
p. 6.

p. 198   Josh Greenfeld, *A Child Called Noah* (New York: Henry Holt,
1972; San Diego: Harcourt Brace Jovanovich, 1988), p. 126.
Christina Baldwin, *Calling the Circle: The First and Future Culture*
(Newberg, OR: Swan*Raven & Company, 1994), p. 47.

p. 199   Anne Lamott, *Bird by Bird: Some Instructions on Writing and Life*
(New York: Pantheon Books, 1994), pp. 191–92.

PART THREE

p. 201   Don Marquis, *the life and times of archy and mehitabel* (Garden
City, NJ: Doubleday, 1950), p. 298.

p. 203   David Remnick, "Reading Japan," *The New Yorker*, 6 February
1995, p. 38.

p. 205   Robert Lindsey, "Surgery Follows Pact on Custody: Down's Syndrome Boy's Case in California Strengthens Rights of Handicapped," *New York Times*, 10 October 1983, sec. A, p. 12.

p. 207   Joseph P. Shapiro, "The Mothers of Invention," *U.S. News and
World Report*, 10 January 1994, p. 42.

p. 208   Vickie Noble, *Down Is Up for Aaron Eagle: A Mother's Spiritual*

Journey with Down Syndrome (New York: HarperCollins, 1993), p. 111.

p. 209   Robert Perske, *Hope for the Families: New Directions for Parents of Persons with Retardation or Other Disabilities* (Nashville: Abingdon Press, 1973), p. 40.

p. 210   E. B. White, *The Trumpet of the Swan* (New York: HarperCollins, 1970; New York: Harper Trophy Book, 1973), p. 170 (page citation is to the reprint edition).

p. 211   Emily Dickinson, #555, *The Complete Poems of Emily Dickinson*, Thomas H. Jackson, ed. (Boston: Little, Brown & Co., 1960), p. 270.

p. 212   John Callahan, *Don't Worry, He Won't Get Far on Foot: The Autobiography of a Dangerous Man* (New York: William Morrow, 1989), p. 120.

p. 214   Anne Lamott, *Bird by Bird: Some Instructions on Writing and Life* (New York: Pantheon Books, 1994), p. 180.

p. 215   Kathleen Norris, *Dakota: A Spiritual Geography* (New York: Ticknor & Fields, 1993), pp. 122, 22, 11.

p. 216   Stephen Mitchell, ed., *The Enlightened Mind: An Anthology of Sacred Prose* (New York: HarperCollins, 1991), p. 115.

p. 218   Annie Dillard, *The Writing Life* (New York: Harper & Row, 1989; New York: Harper Perennial, 1990), p. 32 (page citation is to the reprint edition).

p. 219   Linda Hogan, "Crossings," *The Book of Medicines* (Minneapolis: Coffee House Press, 1993), p. 28. Used by permission of the publisher.
Charles Steinhacker and Susan Flader, *The Sand Country of Aldo Leopold* (San Francisco: Sierra Club, 1973), pp. 17–18.

p. 221   Justin Kaplan, ed., *Bartlett's Familiar Quotations* (Boston: Little, Brown & Co., 1992), p. 610:16.

p. 222   George Judson, "2 Prisoners of History Meet Camera's Captors," *New York Times*, 11 October 1995, sec. B, pp. 1–2.

p. 223   Lewis Carroll, *Through the Looking-Glass* (New York: William Morrow, 1992), p. 267.

p. 224   John Hockenberry, *Moving Violations: War Zones, Wheelchairs, and Declarations of Independence* (New York: Hyperion, 1995), p. 101.

p. 226   Aldo Leopold, *A Sand County Almanac* (New York: Oxford University Press, 1949; New York: Oxford University Press Paperback, 1989), p. 84 (page citation is to the reprint edition).

p. 227   Jerry W. Robinson, Ed. D., et al., *Applied Keyboarding* (Cincinnati, OH: South-Western Publishing Co., 1994), p. 39.

p. 228   P. D. Eastman, *Big Dog . . . Little Dog: A Bedtime Story* (New York: Random House, 1973), last page.

p. 229   Rosellen Brown, preface to *A Voyager Out: A Life of Mary Kingsley,* by Katherine Frank (Boston: Houghton Mifflin Company, 1986), p. xiv.
          Arnold Beisser, *Flying Without Wings: Personal Reflections on Being Disabled* (New York: Doubleday, 1989), p. 187.

p. 230   Gretchen B. Dianda and Betty J. Hofmayer, eds., *Older and Wiser: 716 Memorable Quotes from Those Who Have Lived the Longest and Seen the Most* (New York: Ballantine Books, 1995), p. 132.

p. 231   Olive Ann Burns, *Leaving Cold Sassy* (New York: Ticknor & Fields, 1992), p. 212.

p. 232   Gretchen B. Dianda and Betty J. Hofmayer, eds., *Older and Wiser: 716 Memorable Quotes from Those Who Have Lived the Longest and Seen the Most* (New York: Ballantine Books, 1995), p. 10.

p. 233   Lewis Carroll, *Alice in Wonderland* (New York: William Morrow, 1992), p. 19.
          Henri J. M. Nouwen, *Here and Now: Living in the Spirit* (New York: Crossroad, 1995), p. 45.

p. 235   Ann Landers, *Minneapolis StarTribune,* 20 September 1994.
          Mary Kay Blakely, *Wake Me When It's Over: A Journey to the Edge and Back* (New York: Times Books, 1989), p. 268.

p. 236   Arnold Beisser, *The Only Gift: Thoughts on the Meaning of Friends and Friendship* (New York: Doubleday, 1991), p. 137.

p. 238   Maureen Lynch, *Mary Fran and Mo* (New York: St. Martin's Press, 1979), p. 36.

301

p. 240   Justin Kaplan, ed., *Bartlett's Familiar Quotations* (Boston: Little, Brown & Co., 1992), p. 437:9.

p. 242   "Together We're Better" is the name of a school inclusion project funded by the U.S. Department of Education and jointly implemented by the Minnesota Department of Children, Families, and Learning, and the Institute on Community Integration at the University of Minnesota.

p. 244   Burton Blatt and Fred Kaplan, *Christmas in Purgatory: A Photographic Essay on Mental Retardation* (Syracuse, NY: Human Policy Press, 1974), p. 109.

p. 246   Rosalie Maggio, comp., *The Beacon Book of Quotations by Women* (Boston: Beacon Press, 1992), p. 251.
         Wilson Follett, *Modern American Usage: A Guide*, Jacques Barzun, ed. (New York: Hill & Wang, 1966), p. 12.

p. 248   Virginia DeLand, "One Bite at a Time," in *Making Changes: Family Voices on Living with Disability*, Jan A. Spiegle and Richard van den Pol, eds. (Cambridge, MA: Brookline Books, 1993), p. 94.

p. 250   Andie Tucher, ed., *Bill Moyers: A World of Ideas II* (New York: Doubleday, 1990), p. 40.

p. 251   John Hockenberry, *Moving Violations* (New York: Hyperion, 1995), p. 101.
         Ellen Langer, *Mindfulness* (Reading, MA: Addison-Wesley Publishing Company, 1989; Reading, MA: Addison-Wesley Paperback, 1990), p. 169 (page citation is to the reprint edition).

p. 253   Wilfred Sheed, *In Love with Daylight: A Memoir of Recovery* (New York: Simon & Schuster, 1995), p. 30.

p. 255   Lili Frank Garfinkel, "Adolescent Depression: A Slide into Chaos," *The Pacesetter*, newsletter of the Pacer Center, Minneapolis, MN, February 1995, p. 19.

p. 257   Daniel Goleman, Paul Kaufman, and Michael Ray, *The Creative Spirit* (New York: E. P. Dutton, 1992), p. 38.

p. 259   James R. Oestreich, "When P. D. Q. Meets P. D. Slow," *New York Times*, 1 February 1995, sec. C, p. 6.
         Jay Bobbin, "Off-Broadway on CBS," *TV Week*, magazine of the *Minneapolis StarTribune*, 4 February 1995.

p. 260   John Hockenberry, *Moving Violations* (New York: Hyperion, 1995), p. 5.

p. 264   Christopher Vecsey, *Imagine Ourselves Richly: Mythic Narratives of North American Indians* (New York: HarperCollins, 1991), p. xii. Arnold Beisser, *Flying Without Wings: Personal Reflections on Being Disabled* (New York: Doubleday, 1989), pp. 42–43.

p. 266   Jennie Ladow-Duncan in *From the Heart: On Being the Mother of a Child with Special Needs*, Jayne D. B. Marsh, ed. (Bethesda, MD: Woodbine House, 1995), p. 75.

p. 268   Ellen Langer, *Mindfulness* (Reading, MA: Addison-Wesley Publishing Company, 1989; Reading, MA: Addison-Wesley Paperback, 1990), p. 87 (page citation is to the reprint edition).

p. 269   Cathy McClure, "Happily Ever After?," in *Making Changes: Family Voices on Living with Disabilities*, Jan Spiegle and Richard van den Pol, eds. (Cambridge, MA: Brookline Books, 1993), p. 168. Jane Taylor McDonnell, *News from the Border: A Mother's Memoir of Her Autistic Son* (New York: Ticknor & Fields, 1993), p. 68.

p. 270   Helen Featherstone, *A Difference in the Family: Living with a Disabled Child* (New York: Basic Books, 1980; New York: Penguin Books, 1981), p. 58 (page citation is to the reprint edition).

p. 271   Vickie Noble, *Down Is Up for Aaron Eagle: A Mother's Spiritual Journey with Down Syndrome* (New York: HarperCollins, 1993), p. 52.
Erving Goffman, *Stigma* (New York: Simon & Schuster, 1963; New York: Touchstone, 1986), p. 5 (page citation is to the reprint edition).

p. 273   Fern Kupfer, *Before and After Zachariah: A True Story about a Family and a Different Kind of Courage* (New York: Delacourt, 1982; Chicago: Academy Chicago Publishers, 1982), p. 111 (page citation is to the reprint edition).

p. 278   Sylvia Waugh, *The Mennyms* (New York: Greenwillow Books, 1993), p. 189.

p. 279   Sandra Cisneros, *The House on Mango Street* (Houston: Arte Público Press, 1984; New York: Vintage Books, 1991), p. 75 (page citation is to the reprint edition).

p. 280 Sue Halpern, *Migrations to Solitude* (New York: Pantheon Books, 1992), p. 94.

p. 281 Earl A. Grollman, *Living When a Loved One Has Died,* 2nd ed. (Boston: Beacon Press, 1987), p. 15.

p. 282 Christina Baldwin, *Calling the Circle: The First and Future Culture* (Newberg, OR: Swan*Raven & Company, 1994), p. 43.

p. 284 Stephen Mitchell, ed., *The Enlightened Mind: An Anthology of Sacred Prose* (New York: HarperCollins, 1991), p. 46.

p. 285 Richard C. Anderson, "Walter at 10," in *Uncommon Fathers: Reflections on Raising a Child with a Disability*, Donald J. Meyer, ed. (Bethesda, MD: Woodbine House, 1995), p. 74.

Index of Topics

Acknowledgments

Above all I want to thank any parent, anywhere, who has ever stood up to tell his or her story. Over the years I have heard or spoken with hundreds of parents of children with disabilities—people I met at my son's schools, at conferences and classes, in the course of my work as a consultant and speaker, and in everyday life. Every story I heard has affected me and shaped what I have written in this book. Any success I have had in capturing the diversity of the experience of disability and addressing its universal aspects has been due to this willingness of parents to open their hearts and minds and testify to their experience.

I credit the training I received through the Minnesota Partners in Policymaking program and the Institute for Integrated Education in Montreal for profoundly altering my thinking about disability, community, and social change, and for giving me the chance to meet and learn from courageous leaders in this field.

Many books were important to me in my research, but I am especially indebted to *A Difference in the Family: Living with a Disabled Child* by Helen Featherstone, *Flying Without Wings: Personal Reflections on Being Disabled* by Arnold Beisser, *Stigma* by Erving Goffman, *Mindfulness* by Ellen Langer, and *Walking on Water: Reflections on Faith and Art* by Madeleine L'Engle.

My belief in the tremendous power of invitation was completely confirmed by the generous responses of the many people I asked for help as I wrote this book. I remain touched and humbled by their open giving of their time and expertise. Several people reviewed my proposal for the book and provided valuable suggestions and early encouragement. These include Tom Zirpoli and Jim Kodádek. Over the course of the writing a variety of people served terms on my Sounding Board, reading significant portions of the manuscript, offering insightful comments and personal experiences, and directing me to new resources. My heartfelt thanks go to Jan Grieser, Rita Johnson, Mary Morrow, Sue Hedin, Alison Simons, Heidi Muhs, Sue and Bill Swenson, Doug Westendorp, Mary Jean Babcock, and Marjorie and Richard Roth.

Special thanks are due to Krista Westendorp and Beverly St. John, who read the entire manuscript and responded immediately to each of the many requests I made of them throughout the writing of this book.

Colleen Wieck's enthusiastic support and promotion of this book have been invaluable to me. I am profoundly grateful for all the help she has given so readily.

I thank my yoga teacher, Maryann Parker, for always being there to teach and for her superb articulation of yoga principles, which form the basis for those included in the text. Any deficiency or inaccuracy in these precepts as they appear here is entirely my own.

Many members of my extended family provided various kinds of help and encouragement. I thank each of them, especially my mother, Ellen Delaney, who read the entire manuscript and never flagged in her role as head cheerleader.

I want to give special thanks to the writer Ann Gerike, who was there at the beginning and still there at the end with excellent counsel. Writing teacher Susan Perry gave me the key, and my agent Heide Lange opened the door, to making this book a reality. I am grateful to them both. I am also indebted to my editor, Betsy Lerner, for her patient tutelage of a novice and for her faith in the book; to her assistant, Laura Hodes; and to the copy editor, Frances Apt. Each of them has made this book better.

My sons, Amar and Sam Gill, made many changes in their daily lives and took on new responsibilities to accommodate my writing, and I am proud of them and thankful for their cooperation and support. I relied throughout on the constant strength and help of Harjinder Gill, who gave me not only encouragement but a big, big dictionary and a computer, technical assistance, as well as lots of hugs. He listened to me, praised me, said yes to whatever I asked, and, not least, paid the bills.

It takes a long time to write a book and most of it is solitary, even lonely, work. I offer deep thanks to those relatives, friends, and acquaintances, too numerous to mention here, whose steady interest and encouragement were daily bread to me.

About the Author

Barbara Gill is an attorney and disability consultant. The mother of two sons, one of whom has Down syndrome, she has served on many disability related boards and committees, including four years as a board member of her local Arc. A former Special Assistant Attorney General for Minnesota, she began her career working in the fields of mental health, welfare, and criminal law. She is a graduate of Minnesota Partners in Policymaking and the Montreal Institute for Integrated Education. She lives with her family in Minneapolis.